Promoting Social Skills
in the Inclusive Classroom

WHAT WORKS FOR SPECIAL-NEEDS LEARNERS

Karen R. Harris and Steve Graham, *Editors*

www.guilford.com/WWFSNL

This series addresses a significant need in the education of students who are at risk, those with disabilities, and all children and adolescents who struggle with learning or behavior. While researchers in special education, educational psychology, curriculum and instruction, and other fields have made great progress in understanding what works for struggling learners, the practical application of this research base remains quite limited. Books in the series present assessment, instructional, and classroom management methods that have strong empirical evidence. Written in a user-friendly format, each volume provides specific how-to instructions and examples of the use of proven procedures in schools. Coverage is sufficiently thorough and detailed to enable practitioners to implement the practices described; many titles include reproducible practical tools. Recent titles have Web pages where purchasers can download and print the reproducible materials.

Promoting Social Skills in the Inclusive Classroom

Kimber L. Wilkerson
Aaron B. T. Perzigian
Jill K. Schurr

THE GUILFORD PRESS
New York   London

© 2014 The Guilford Press
A Division of Guilford Publications, Inc.
72 Spring Street, New York, NY 10012
www.guilford.com

Printed in the United States of America

This book is printed on acid-free paper.

Last digit is print number: 9 8 7 6 5 4 3 2 1

Library of Congress Cataloging-in-Publication Data

Wilkerson, Kimber L.
  Promoting social skills in the inclusive classroom / Kimber L. Wilkerson, Aaron B. T.
Perzigian, Jill K. Schurr.
    pages cm. — (What works for special-needs learners)
  Includes bibliographical references and index.
  ISBN 978-1-4625-1148-8 (pbk.) — ISBN 978-1-4625-1171-6 (hardcover)
  1. Inclusive education—Social aspects—United States.   2. Social skills—Study
and teaching (Elementary)—United States.   I. Perzigian, Aaron B. T.   II. Schurr,
Jill K.   III. Title.
  LC1201.W55 2014
  371.9'0460973—dc23
                                                              2013021678

About the Authors

Kimber L. Wilkerson, PhD, is Professor of Special Education and Chair of the Department of Rehabilitation Psychology and Special Education at the University of Wisconsin–Madison. Before earning her doctorate, Dr. Wilkerson was a special educator in a day treatment program for students with emotional and behavioral disorders and cotaught in an inclusive elementary school program. She has published and presented on topics such as providing instruction to students in alternative settings and combining academic with social skills instruction—particularly in the area of reading. She also has experience providing both inservice and preservice instruction to increase the capacity of teachers to meet the academic and social skills needs of students with learning and behavioral disorders.

Aaron B. T. Perzigian, MS, is a full-time graduate student pursuing his doctorate in the Department of Rehabilitation Psychology and Special Education at the University of Wisconsin–Madison. Mr. Perzigian is licensed to teach middle and high school English. Prior to graduate school, he worked as an English teacher and cross-categorical special educator in a residential treatment setting. His research interests include alternative education, dropout prevention, and social competence development for children and adolescents with disabilities.

Jill K. Schurr, PhD, is Professor of Psychology at Austin College in Sherman, Texas. Dr. Schurr has developed partnerships with local schools and psychological clinics to promote the increased implementation of positive behavioral interventions and supports (PBIS) programs and availability of applied behavior analysis services in the community. Before earning her doctorate, she was a middle school teacher at an alternative school and worked as a research assistant on the Multimodal Treatment of ADHD study sponsored by the National Institute of Mental Health, providing interventions for children with attention-deficit/hyperactivity disorder. Dr. Schurr has published and presented on topics such as academic learning time, using a PBIS model to improve outcomes for students with emotional and behavioral disorders, and professional development to increase teachers' use of behavior strategies in the classroom.

Acknowledgments

We would first like to thank Karen R. Harris, Mary Emily Warner Professor in the Mary Lou Fulton Teachers College at Arizona State University and coeditor of the What Works for Special-Needs Learners series, for her encouragement and support in bringing this volume to fruition. Karen's thoughtfulness, high standards, and keen intellect leave a mark on all her projects and the people who are lucky enough to be involved with them. We would also like to thank Rochelle Serwator, Senior Editor at The Guilford Press, for her patience, flexibility, helpful suggestions, and skillful shepherding. Mary Beth Anderson, Editorial Assistant at Guilford, also deserves thanks for her competence, clarity, and thorough attention in helping transform the manuscript into a book.

Catherine R. Lark deserves special thanks for her assistance with Chapter 3. Catherine's hard work researching programs and finding sources that were not always easy to track down allowed us to make sure we had all of the information we needed to accurately evaluate each program. Additionally, we appreciate Catherine's patience and diligence in summarizing the program descriptions. It took several iterations to find the structure that would work for all the different schoolwide programs, and Catherine responded to each revision request with her usual "No problem!" and a smile.

Jennifer L. Schroeder also deserves special thanks for her assistance with Chapter 6. When it became apparent that the information originally outlined for one chapter should be expanded across two, Jennifer stepped in with her usual efficiency. Her input on and examples of individual assessment strategies were invaluable.

We would also like to thank Ms. Kari Steck for graciously sharing her lesson plans to incorporate into the book. Ms. Steck is one example of the bright, energetic teachers who remind us that the teaching profession attracts impressive talent.

Finally, we want to acknowledge the many students and teachers we have worked with over the years who continue to motivate our interest in improving the social lives of students in inclusive classrooms.

Contents

CHAPTER 1

The Importance of Social Skills

As educators, how do we determine that a student is successful in elementary school? One obvious measure of academic success in an elementary school classroom is academic achievement. Following from that, one fairly well-accepted measure of academic achievement is the assessment of students' mastery of grade-level content via standardized tests. For example, a third grader is successful if proficient on tests that assess mastery of the third-grade language arts, math, science, and social studies content covered in the approved curriculum. Of course, educators often make the case that there are other ways to measure success in school. In many instances, other suggested measures of success include objectives that are more difficult to quantify: the ability to apply content and skills learned in school to real-world problems, feelings of self-efficacy as a learner, civic engagement, or even a sense of acceptance and belonging. Regardless of the definition of academic success used, the premise of this book is that fostering and promoting social competence among students will enhance their success in school.

In inclusive classrooms—that is, classrooms in which students with disabilities are educated alongside their peers without disabilities—it is often students with disabilities who experience compromised academic achievement. These students are also more likely than their peers without disabilities to be viewed as less socially skilled than their classmates and to be less socially accepted—both by their peers and their teachers. Inclusive education has been promoted for over 25 years as a way to increase the academic achievement and social status of elementary students with disabilities. As far back as the Regular Education Initiative (REI) in 1985, including students with disabilities in general education classrooms with their same-age peers has been pro-moted as a viable, if not morally necessary, option for improving the stubbornly per-sistent poor postschool outcomes that students with disabilities continue to experience. It is up to classroom teachers, however, to provide instruction—through pedagogical choices and curricular adoptions and adaptations—that fosters success. This book pro-vides a rationale for focusing on social competence in the elementary classroom and clarifies some of the differences in conceptions of what characteristics and behaviors make up one's social competence. In later chapters, we also provide descriptions of interventions and strategies stemming from those various conceptions that can be used to enhance and promote social competence as a way to bolster success. We start with a brief summary of the research base linking social competence to academic success.

RESEARCH BASE

Research demonstrates that social skills—and the social competence afforded by mas-tery of social skills—are important mediators of academic success. That is, a student's social competence has an impact, albeit indirect, on his or her academic achievement. As a striking example of this, social competence in the third grade has been shown to predict academic achievement in the eighth grade above and beyond (i.e., "controlling for") third-grade achievement (Caprara, Barbaranelli, Pastorelli, Bandura, & Zimbardo, 2000). This research reminds us that if our goals as educators of elementary school students include lasting and continuous academic achievement, then we must attend to our students' social competence as well as their mastery of academic skills and knowl-edge. Attention to social competence should be considered not simply as a way to man-age behavior and promote smooth operation of the classroom setting but also as a way to maximize achievement.

Considering that students with disabilities in elementary school classrooms are often identified as having poor social skills and are generally less well accepted than their typically developing peers, it is also important to note that the relationship between social competence and academic success can be both positive or negative; research reveals that social competence—or lack thereof—predicts both positive and negative academic outcomes for students (Bursuck & Asher, 1986; Kupersmidt, Coie, & Dodge, 1990; Parker & Asher, 1987; Ray & Elliott, 2006; Wentzel, 1993; Wilson, Pianta, & Stuhl-man, 2007). On the positive end of the spectrum, research has linked school-related social competence with longer term adult, nonschool outcomes (Gest, Sesma, Masten, & Tellegen, 2006; McDougall, Hymel, Vaillancourt, & Mercer, 2001; Parker, Rubin, Price, & De Rosier, 1995). In academic domains, for example, social competence is associated with school success across grades and ability levels; social competence predicts grade promotion, high school completion, and participation in postsecondary education. In fact, in some seminal research, characteristics, and behaviors thought to reflect social competence were found to be more predictive of some academic achievements than tests of cognitive ability (Lambert, 1972; Feldhusen, Thurston, & Benning, 1970).

On the other end of the continuum, an absence of social competence can be predic-tive of school failure. Grade retention, disability status, experience with disciplinary action, and school dropout are a few of the numerous negative outcomes associated with underdeveloped social competence (Kupersmidt & Coie, 1990). Moreover, employment patterns, delinquency, and civic participation in adulthood are related to the social competence skills acquired and demonstrated by students throughout the school years.

From all this, we conclude that social competence matters. Next, we summarize the importance and role of social competence in inclusive classrooms, where students with disabilities are educated alongside their peers, and underscore the importance of positive peer interactions in those settings. This is followed by a brief description of two pathways through which social competence is linked to academic success. We conclude this chapter with a brief description of specific social skills that have been shown over time to be valued by classroom teachers.

SOCIAL COMPETENCE IN THE INCLUSIVE CLASSROOM

Inclusive education, or the participation of students with disabilities in the classrooms of their same-aged peers without disabilities, relies heavily—in theory and in practice—on successful social interactions among students across ability levels. Classroom tasks in inclusive classrooms commonly include activities built on interaction and engagement with peers. This shift in pedagogy is based in part on teachers' desire to build on the strengths that heterogeneous classrooms afford. The greater use of peer-mediated and cooperative forms of instruction also reflects educators' responses to the changing demands of success in the workplace where group problem solving, building upon the ideas of others, and sharing resources are associated with greater gains, more efficiency, and better outcomes. Working and learning with others necessarily involves talking, questioning, compromising and even arguing. Students who can navigate these tasks well are in a good position to be successful in school and beyond.

In order to prepare students for that success—in postsecondary school settings and the workplace—and give them the skills they will need to function in a global economy, educators often use a variety of forms of peer-mediated instruction. Peer-mediated instruction includes such techniques as cooperative learning groups, peer tutoring, and "team" approaches to task completion as well as variations of peer editing/feedback. All of these peer-mediated pedagogical tools require students to interact with their peers around academic tasks as the means to honing their academic skills. For many students, this is a "win–win"; both academic and social skills increase. However, not all students can easily navigate interactions with their peers to benefit academically. For instance, students with disabilities are subject to higher rates of peer rejection and negative self-perceptions than students without disabilities (Nowicki, 2003).

Indeed, disability status during childhood increases the risk of victimization (e.g., being bullied at school) (Thompson, Whitney, & Smith, 1994; Whitney, Nabuzoka, & Smith, 1992). Poor social skills, which frequently coexist with disability status, prevent many students from positive peer engagement, which thus hinders them from reaping the benefits of peer-mediated instruction. It makes sense, therefore, that teachers who value peer interaction are drawn to learning more about improving the social skills, social competence, and social acceptance of students with disabilities.

PEER REJECTION: THE OTHER EXTREME

While promoting social competence is valued for academic and postschool success, at the other end of the continuum, a lack of social competence can inhibit social acceptance, which can thus result in harm. For example, having little to no social circle, which can be dependent on one's social competence, is linked to higher rates of school disengagement, social rejection, and even victimization, all of which are associated with lower rates of self-esteem and higher rates of depression-like symptoms. Indeed, the combination of social skills deficits and disability labels can endorse various forms of peer rejection, which predicts experiences of bullying, alienation, and the associated consequences. Thus, a chain reaction of rejection, mediated by social competence difficulties, influences many of the negative academic and social outcomes experienced by students with disabilities.

It probably comes as no surprise that childhood rejection increases one's risk of dropout, adult unemployment, and maladjustment (Vaughn, Haager, Hogan, & Kouzekanani, 1992). Furthermore, rejection by peers during a student's younger years often remains a constant lived experience through adulthood (Vaughn, McIntosh, & Spencer-Rowe, 1991). One way to change patterns of rejection for students with disabilities is to address social skills development in an intentional way in elementary schools. Additionally, providing frequent opportunities for positive interaction between students with disabilities and their peers can help replace peers' negative social perceptions of students with disabilities, which play a substantial role in rejection status (Hastings & Graham, 1995; Whitaker, 1994) and ultimately lead to poor academic achievement. In Chapter 5, we further elaborate the benefits of peer mediated, small-group instruction on both academic and social goals, and provide examples of evidence-based practices in peer-mediated instruction that teachers can employ in inclusive classrooms. These techniques are one way to address the social difficulties sometimes faced by students with disabilities and improve, overall, the social competence of all classroom members.

PATHWAYS CONNECTING SOCIAL COMPETENCE TO ACADEMIC SUCCESS

Most teachers do not have to be convinced of the important connection between social competence and academic success. They have seen the relationship play out in their classrooms on a regular basis. However, when pressed to explain the processes underlying that connection, teachers may default to intuition or common sense. Teachers may even wonder: Why do the underlying processes matter? Isn't it enough to know that social skills are important and to foster them?

We believe that consideration of the underlying processes *is* important if we are going to make inroads. In this section, we describe two specific pathways through which social competence is thought to affect academic achievement. The first involves mastery and demonstration of skills we refer to as "academic enablers." The second pathway is through perception: A student's self-perception of social competence as well as peers' and teachers' perception of that student's social competence is thought to play a role in achievement. For educators interested in promoting social competence, under-standing these pathways is important to help guide decision making about pedagogy and curriculum. Understanding these pathways should prove helpful for teachers in prioritizing experiences and activities in the classroom on a day-to-day basis.

Social Skills as Academic Enablers

Part of being socially competent is mastery of specific social skills sets. Social skills are valuable in a wide range of settings. In learning environments, specific social skills can be thought of as "academic enablers." Academic enablers are attitudes and behaviors (e.g., motivation and strong interpersonal skills) that facilitate student learning (DiPerna & Elliott, 2002). Having a high level of social knowledge—that is, knowing what to do and when to do it in school contexts (Bursuck & Asher, 1986)—is one example of a social skill that is an academic enabler. When students in elementary school classrooms demonstrate a high level of social knowledge, they generally experience the approval of their peers and teachers. Teacher and peer approval is, in turn, paramount to the school success of students both with and without disabilities as it affords membership in the overall identity of the school. Students with disabilities, however, often feel less connected to their school and report lower feelings of belonging to the school com-munity than their peers without disabilities. Following this logic, competence in social knowledge—that is, knowing what to do when—is directly related to school attach-ment, which is then related to student achievement.

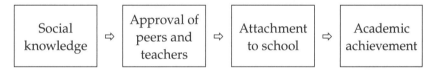

Considering this process allows teachers to think about multiple points of entry for impacting a student's academic achievement. Certainly, directly targeting academic achievement through directly teaching academic skills and abilities is prudent. How-ever, we argue that targeting social knowledge is equally important to academic success. Additionally, understanding the links allows educators to consider the other important processes at work. Increasing social knowledge should result in higher rates of approval by peers and teachers, but educators who are aware of this path can also make addi-tional efforts to foster acceptance and approval. Likewise, a savvy educator will also be on the lookout for ways to increase students' attachment to school—all in the service of promoting academic achievement in the present as well as in years to come.

Perceptions of Social Competence

A second pathway connecting social competence to academic success is through percep-tions. The ways in which peers perceive a fellow student's social abilities, for example, is central to the social status of that student. In this regard, the social capabilities—or deficits or idiosyncrasies—that elementary students display in school settings are associated with popularity or rejection among peers (Coie, Dodge, & Coppotelli, 1982). Similarly, social behavior in the classroom impacts the reputation a student develops with adults in a school. A positive reputation among teachers may afford individual students opportunities that may otherwise not exist. For example, teachers who perceive specific students to be more socially capable than others are more likely to place additional value in (e.g., grant approval to) those students. That approval can translate into more and higher quality attention from those teachers.

Not only do the perceptions of others affect a student's overall social competence, but a student's self-perception of his or her social competence also affects acceptance by others, adding to the web of connections.

| Self-perception of social competence | ⇨ | Peer and teacher perception of social competence | ⇨ | Approval of peers and teachers |

Some researchers have suggested that the social skills capacity of students is rooted in how well they believe their responses to social tasks are received by others (see Gresham, 1992). In this case, "social tasks" includes all manner of interactions with teachers and peers that take place in school environments. For example, social responses that are required for completion of collaborative group work with peers and reactions to teacher directives are forms of interaction through which students can gauge the efficacy of their own social competence. Students who perceive their social participation as strong and capable are more likely to exhibit confidence and develop friendships with peers, thus minimizing opportunities for social rejection. Additionally, positive self-perception increases one's self-esteem, which allows for a comfortable existence in learning environments, thereby increasing attachment to school.

Students with negative self-perceptions of their social abilities are less likely to initiate interactions with peers and participate in group activities unprompted, in effect closing themselves to friendships and traditionally valued acceptance. Furthermore, a displayed lack of confidence can deter peers from initiating contact or inviting participation in various activities. Academically, students who are perceived to be lacking in self-confidence are less likely to work collaboratively with peers and to thus reap the benefits of peer-mediated instruction and authentic cooperative learning.

SOCIAL SKILLS VALUED BY TEACHERS

Social skills are often described as a set of abilities that enable children to respond in acceptable ways to certain social requests (Elliott & McKinnie, 1994). In a classroom setting, social requests often come from teachers. Research has shown that elementary school teachers consistently value certain classroom social skills and even require them in their classrooms. For example, teachers, by and large, expect students to attend to and follow directions, request assistance in appropriate ways, ignore peer distractions, and manage conflicts with peers and adults (Hersh & Walker, 1983; Kerr & Zigmond, 1986; Lane, Pierson, & Givner, 2003). Teachers also expect students to demonstrate self-control and cooperation skills (Gresham, Dolstra, Lambros, McLaughlin, & Lane, 2000; Lane, Givner, & Pierson, 2004; Lane, Pierson, & Givner, 2004). Often teachers' classroom demands reflect an expectation that these skills are acquired and demonstrated in a variety of everyday situations. In sum, these expectations represent a set of high-level social skills. These skills and behaviors are good examples of "academic enablers" described earlier in this chapter; when combined with academic content competence, these skills form a pathway to academic success.

SUMMARY, CONCLUSION, AND WHAT'S AHEAD

In this opening chapter, we introduced social competence as a set of skills that allow students to meet the various academic and social expectations of an elementary classroom, a concept we explore further in the chapters to come. Students with disabilities often display lower levels of social competence than their peers and, therefore, often experience compromised academic and social outcomes. The link between social competence and academic achievement is strong—so strong, in fact, that those students perceived as socially competent individuals, regardless of disability status, are more likely to reach many short- and long-term educational goals (e.g., grade promotion, graduation, and postsecondary schooling). Thus, it is imperative for elementary educators in inclusive settings to emphasize the learning and practice of social competencies so that students with and without disabilities alike are more prepared for school and postschool success. The following is a list of major points introduced in this chapter:

- ✓ Social competence is a strong mediator of academic success.
- ✓ A student's level of social competence in the early grades can predict both immediate and future school achievements and long-term adult outcomes.
- ✓ Inclusive education relies heavily—both in theory and in practice—on successful social interactions between students with and without disabilities.
- ✓ Peer-mediated instruction, a concept expanded upon in Chapter 5, is a commonly used instructional strategy that facilitates peer interaction in inclusive settings.
- ✓ Students with disabilities experience higher rates of social rejection, which is thus linked to higher rates of school disengagement and dropout.
- ✓ Providing authentic classroom opportunities for students with disabilities to develop and practice social competencies with their peers reduces and prevents social rejection.
- ✓ Social competence can influence academic achievement through two pathways: "academic enablers" and perception.
- ✓ "Social knowledge"—or knowing what to do and when in the classroom environment—is an example of an academic enabler.

✓ Having a positive reputation among teachers and peers—or being perceived favorably—is an example of perception as a pathway to academic achievement.

✓ The social skills associated with social competence can be thought of as knowing how to respond to academic and social requests; perhaps the most necessary skill set for succeeding in school.

In later chapters, we describe evidence-based interventions and strategies that teachers can employ in inclusive classrooms as well as schoolwide interventions that can support teachers' efforts to foster and enhance social competence. While the strategies and interventions described would be of value in the education of all students—as befits a book devoted to ideas for use in inclusive classrooms—we pay particular attention to strategies and interventions that promise to address the needs of students with disabilities in those classrooms.

Chapter 2 provides a summary of the variety of ways that social competence has been conceptualized and the student characteristics and behaviors through which social competence is displayed. This summary is meant to draw attention to the complexity of the concept we refer to as "social competence" throughout this book. Social competence can be conceptualized theoretically in a variety of ways, which plays out in interventions that are developed for use in elementary schools and classrooms. The remaining chapters are devoted to describing interventions that have promise, or a strong evidence base, for their use in inclusive elementary classrooms. In Chapter 3, we provide a summary of schoolwide approaches to bolstering social competence, while in Chapter 4, we address the question of "What is evidence-based practice?" and summarize a number social skill interventions appropriate for use in the general education classroom. In Chapter 5, we present effective forms of peer-mediated instruction and the elements of group work that are most closely associated with social benefits for students that teachers can weave into their instruction. In Chapter 6, we identify and describe a number of methods for assessing an individual student's social skills needs. To conclude, in Chapter 7, we outline components of evidence-based individual intervention plans, including a summary of strategies appropriate to use with individual students—those with particularly intractable or unique social skill difficulties—within an inclusive setting. It is our hope that this book will give educators ample ideas, strategies, and insights needed to continue to value, prioritize, and enhance the social competence of the students they serve.

CHAPTER 2

The Wide and Varied Definitions of Social Competence

As we established in Chapter 1, success in school hinges in many ways on how well students are able to navigate the academic and social demands of a classroom environment. We acknowledge that social competence provides students with a variety of academic, social, and personal skills, which help them to meet and sometimes exceed the many expectations imposed by peers and teachers. For example, socially competent students are typically viewed more positively and are thus able to access social opportunities that may not be granted to students perceived to be lacking social competence. Furthermore, students who are considered socially competent have higher levels of self-esteem and self-confidence, are more engaged in school activities, and have better academic and long-term adult outcomes compared with those who are socially isolated or even rejected within the school environment as a result of social difficulties.

It is important to acknowledge that many different personal and social characteristics and behaviors are considered when evaluating a student's social competence; a universal recipe of what makes someone socially competent isn't typically recognized. Rather, in many circumstances, a student is thought to be socially competent if he or she embodies various prosocial traits, which are often dependent upon the context in which the student resides. We discuss various ways to measure social competence in Chapter 6; some of the methods, such as rating scales, do have specific characteristics and behaviors that the evaluator assesses and measures but are not necessarily universally reflective of all the ways social competence is conceptualized. Thus, as educators, we must keep in mind that the meaning of social competence is flexible, is interpreted differently across settings and measurement tools, and includes a variety of personal characteristics and behaviors that are considered to predict positive academic and social outcomes.

Although the composition of social competence can be understood in multiple ways, it is generally accepted that a socially competent student is one who exemplifies various prosocial characteristics (e.g., follows rules; is helpful, compassionate, patient, and polite) in the school environment. These traits, when evaluated individually, are often regarded as independent behaviors, which is important to note because many understandings and interpretations of social competence incorporate various combinations of independent behaviors. Thus, social competence is frequently conceptualized, or viewed, as a smorgasbord of positive and socially valued behaviors. The exact combination of which behaviors to include in one evaluation and not another is, in many instances, determined by the imposing judge (e.g., teacher, researcher, or school psychologist) or tool of measurement (e.g., rating scale).

By being aware of various ways that social competence is understood and interpreted in school settings, educators are able to consider the various social competencies that can be promoted in the classroom and the ways in which these competencies can be taught. In this chapter, we present student personal and social characteristics and behaviors that are interpreted as components of social competence within the context of a school environment. We have created five tables, organized by theme, to help visualize components of social competence in certain developmental areas: social competence as (1) a general characteristic, (2) an academic enabler, (3) a component of socioemotional competence, (4) a psychological construct, and (5) a component of social skills. It is interesting to note that while not all characteristics and behaviors presented under each theme are independently labeled as social competencies specifically, researchers and practitioners alike consider them paramount abilities in students' repertoires of social skills, which, as many argue, is essentially students' social competence.

THE MANY INTERPRETATIONS OF SOCIAL COMPETENCE

As a general trait, social competence largely reflects students' abilities to meet a variety of basic classroom expectations (e.g., follow directions, work collaboratively with peers, and stay on task). In other words, the overall level of students' social competence can be understood as a set of discrete social skills they have mastered that then allows them to satisfy basic, everyday demands of the school environment. Elementary classroom teachers routinely reinforce general socially competent behavior as well as teach and reinforce specific social skills. For example, cooperation skills are often expected and reinforced in elementary classrooms through basic group work learning strategies or group play. As noted in Chapter 1, many explicit social skills, such as following directions and cooperating with peers, can be referred to as "academic enablers." Although they may not involve actual academic ability, these skills heighten a student's chances for academic success in the classroom by way of social experiences.

In the remainder of this chapter, we describe various characteristics and behaviors indicative of a student's social competence. It is our hope that by reflecting upon multiple ways of conceptualizing social competence we can better understand our own interpretations of prosocial school behaviors and how these interpretations affect the ways we perceive students as well as influence the social skills we choose to promote and teach in our classrooms.

Social Competence as General School Participation Characteristics

In this section, we describe social competence as a reflection of common school participation processes. Thinking about social competence as a general school participation characteristic means stepping out of the traditional social skills framework and examining the school participation processes that both reflect and foster positive social and academic experiences. Here we highlight three specific examples of school participation processes—belonging, resiliency, and school readiness—that play a significant role in the acquisition, maintenance, and demonstration of social competence. Thinking about social competence as mediated through common school participation processes allows us to frame social skills in a larger school context. In many instances, social skills are cited in a framework that focuses on immediate student–peer or student–teacher situations; sometimes our thinking about the scope of influence of social competence and platforms upon which it can develop is limited. Thus, using a process-focused lens reminds us that building social competencies into our classroom environment has consequences that transcend the classroom and are, in fact, embedded within the overall schooling experiences of our students. Following are examples of three general school participation processes that can be viewed as indicators of social competence.

Sense of Belonging

There are multiple mechanisms through which students are able to navigate their classrooms and other school settings (e.g., library, lunchroom, playground). In many circumstances, students rely upon various mechanisms, or personal and social factors, for helping them make choices that will lead to academic or social opportunities that precede positive outcomes. In the example of students who engage in common niceties (e.g., saying "please" and "thank you") and are viewed as courteous and well mannered, the act of being polite can be interpreted as a mechanism that facilitates successful relationship building and thus reflects a certain level of social competence.

As a general trait—or process—social competence can be viewed as a confluence of mechanisms that help students be successful in a variety of academic and social situations. School attachment, one such mechanism by which social competencies are mediated, is the process that encourages and permits students to participate fully in a learning setting and enjoy the academic and social experiences they encounter. In a school context, attachment is described as the sense of belonging and connectedness that students feel toward staff, peers, and the academic and social climate (e.g., curricula and physical classroom spaces). Generally, school attachment is understood as the total comfort level students experience while immersed in their learning environment.

A connection, or comfort, with school can be an initial step toward establishing personal affiliation with the learning process. Subsequently, an individual's identification with learning and self-perception of belonging in the school environment is indicative of the confidence levels with which he or she approaches academic and social opportunities. Confidence, itself a stand-alone characteristic of social competence, can, in turn, significantly affect one's academic and social performance. Thus, relative to our discussion of mechanisms that help students in academic and social endeavors, confidence can be considered one such mechanism that facilitates academic and social risk taking.

Theorists and researchers in education and related fields indicate that the various domains of attachment and mechanisms such as friendship and belonging, which facilitate areas of school attachment, can influence higher academic achievement and social participation (Ainsworth, 1973, 1979; Bergin & Bergin, 2009; Bowlby, 1969; Bretherton & Munholland, 1999; Zsolnai, 2002). Thus, students who perform at expected academic levels and participate appropriately in the social environment of the classroom, which can be mediated through the agencies of school attachment, are generally perceived as socially competent individuals. In the chapters to come, we describe strategies and interventions that are designed, in part, to increase students' feelings of attachment to school and thereby their social competence.

Resiliency

Another way to view social competence is through the lens of resiliency, or as an individual's capacity to overcome obstacles or barriers to success (Benard, 1993; Kirby & Fraser, 1997; Masten, 1994; Wang, Haertel, & Walberg, 1997; Wright & Masten, 2005). Social competence viewed from a resiliency framework means thinking about students' social competence as a reflection of protective factors that help them navigate the academic and social expectations of a school setting, especially in spite of barriers or risk factors. For example, students with language difficulties may encounter some communication disadvantages in classroom settings. Thus, language or communication hurdles can be considered risk factors that may become barriers to achievement. Resiliency, in this example, is the ability to be successful in a whole-class inclusive setting despite instruction that relies heavily on communication and language skills. Thus, the capacity to negotiate any complications—or barriers—that arise as a result of language difficulties can be interpreted as part of the students' social competence.

Meeting academic and social expectations and following classroom routines while faced with obstacles (in the case of our example, language barriers) is an indication of students' social competence (Conduct Problems Prevention Research Group, 1999; Denham, 2006; La Paro & Pianta, 2000; Shonkoff & Phillips, 2000). In other words, social competence can be thought of as a confluence of protective factors (e.g., school attachment, self-confidence, assertiveness) that facilitate prosocial behavior and academic achievement in a variety of situations. However, it can be difficult to interpret whether social competence is resiliency or if it is operationalized as the process of attachment, since resiliency is often a result of attachment. As educators, it is important to reflect upon the ways in which we conceptualize the various processes in which students are engaged so that we are aware of what and how certain behaviors are promoted and valued in our classroom.

School Readiness

While resiliency is an important component of a student's education, some may contend that resiliency in a school setting cannot be achieved without a certain "readiness" to be in that environment. Thus, social competence can also be broadly defined as school readiness (Denham, 2006; Hampton & Fantuzzo, 2003). From this perspective, measures of social competence involve students' capacity for regulating personal behaviors and emotions, their level of expressiveness, and the degree to which they participate in social situations. Individuals are thus considered ready to learn when these traits are demonstrated. Similarly, students' general approach to learning, including self-control, classroom interpersonal skills, and internalized and externalized behaviors, reflects an overall level of social competence (Galindo & Fuller, 2010). In later chapters, we highlight effective instructional practices that are designed to enhance the social skills that fall under the school readiness umbrella (e.g., self-control, everyday prosocial classroom behaviors). See Table 2.1 for further components of social competence as a general and wide-encompassing characteristic.

TABLE 2.1. General Components and Participation Processes of Students' Social Competence

For further reference	Components
Ainsworth (1973, 1979); Bergin & Bergin (2009); Bowlby (1969); Bretherton & Munholland (1999); Zsolnai (2002)	Attachment to school, attachment to peers, attachment to family
Benard (1993); Kirby & Fraser (1997); Masten (1994); Wang et al. (1997); Wright & Masten (2005)	Combined protective factors, process of resiliency
Conduct Problems Prevention Research Group (1999); Denham (2006); La Paro & Pianta (2000); Shonkoff & Phillips (2000)	Ability to meet the collective academic and social demands of school, following routines
Dreeben (1968); Jackson (1968)	Dependability, punctuality, and obedience during the learning process
Denham (2006); Hampton & Fantuzzo (2003)	School readiness—ability to regulate personal behavior and emotions, expressiveness, and social participation
Galindo & Fuller (2010)	Approaches to learning, self-control, interpersonal skills, internalized problem behaviors, and externalized behaviors
Wentzel & Caldwell (1997); Wentzel (1991)	Socioemotional well-being

Social Competence as Academic Proficiency

In school settings, social competence is sometimes defined as mastery of a set of social skills and abilities that are relevant and even necessary for meeting academic expectations. We presented a few of these specific skills in Chapter 1 as "academic enablers." For instance, social competence can be a reflection of a student's academic effort, or the level of determination with which that student completes his or her coursework (Bernard, 1995). Comparably, social competence can be interpreted simply as an indication of one's academic reputation; some research indicates that higher academic achievement affords students greater access to friendships and peer popularity (Brown, 1989; Brown & Lohr, 1987). Put in other words: Students would rather associate with and befriend peers who do well in school. Thus, school achievement is a pathway to friendship and social desirability.

Indeed, discussed briefly in Chapter 1 as part of a pathway through which social competence emerges, a good academic reputation often grants to students a certain type of social acceptance among both teachers and peers. Students who perform well academically are held in higher esteem by teachers and classmates and are thus more well liked and awarded higher social status, which provides access to the social environment (Brown, 1989). In turn, access to the social environment improves one's overall attachment to school, an interpretation and mechanism of social competence itself.

There are multiple academic and social implications of popularity and social acceptance in school contexts, one of which is access to opportunities that may not be available to all students. For example, students who are well liked typically receive more individual attention from teachers (e.g., extra assistance) and may be more likely to receive teacher nominations for desirable classroom posts (e.g., teacher helper). Also, being well-liked engenders high expectations among teachers, which is typically accompanied by increased positive behaviors and higher academic achievements. Regarding peer friendship, popularity among fellow classmates may permit membership in various social clubs and activities, which, in turn, increases that student's attachment and feelings of belonging to the school environment.

While educators do not typically set out to increase students' popularity, it is important to consider the link between academic achievements, being well liked, increased self-confidence, and being perceived as socially competent. Students with disabilities often lag behind their peers without disabilities on measures of all these attributes (see Nowicki, 2003; Roberts & Zubrick, 1993; Simeonsson, Carlson, Huntington, McMillen, & Brent, 2001; Wagner, Newman, Cameto, Levine, & Marder, 2007). Therefore, general educators in inclusive classrooms must be especially cognizant of the social experiences of students with disabilities and aware of ways in which their academic and social experiences and competencies can be improved. See Table 2.2 for additional academic-focused components of social competence.

Social Competence as Socioemotional Competence

Social competence can also be interpreted as the result of emotional competence, which includes the personal characteristics of emotional regulation and awareness (see Elias

TABLE 2.2. Academic Components of Students' Social Competence

For further reference	Components
Bernard (1995)	Academic effort
Brown (1989); Brown & Lohr (1987)	Academic reputation
Curby et al. (2008)	Ability to stay engaged and complete assigned tasks
Fantuzzo et al. (2004)	Attitude toward learning
Ladd & Burgress (1999); Rimm-Kaufman et al. (2000); Sieber (1979); Wilson et al. (2007)	Following academic-related directions
McClelland et al. (2006)	Learning-related skills

& Haynes, 2008; Saarni, 1999, 2007). Emotional regulation is the ability to control the behaviors that result from various emotional states (e.g., yelling when angry, crying when upset). Emotional awareness is the understanding of one's personal emotions and the ensuing ability to recognize them and respond to them appropriately (e.g., knowing triggers of frustration and taking the necessary steps to decompress). From this perspective, the recognition and regulation of emotions is believed to be the core of developing positive relationships with peers and teachers. The link between emotional competence and social competence is that positive relationships influence an individual's social experiences. Thus, without emotional control, social relationships are difficult—if not impossible—to build and maintain, and a student's social experiences may not reflect competence.

It should be noted that interpreting social competence with a focus on emotions can be considered a hybrid interpretation. Through this lens, social skills are not independent of emotional competence. For example, it may be insufficient for educators to think about social competence without first considering a student's emotional well-being. Indeed, one's positive social experiences are often grounded by his or her emotional stability. Some students with disabilities, particularly those with emotional and behavioral disorders, are especially prone to emotional instability and often struggle with regulating emotions. Thus, it is not uncommon for many students with disabilities to experience difficulty in social situations because of an inability to control their outward display of emotional behavior.

In addition to recognizing and regulating personal emotions, being able to read and respond appropriately to others' feelings and behaviors is a critical factor in whether a student is perceived as socially competent (Seifer, Gouley, Miller, & Zakriski, 2004). Although emotional regulation can simply be considered a character trait independent of social competence, it can also be interpreted as a socioemotional characteristic prerequisite to developing social competence. In this regard, emotional regulation is at the core of social competence insofar as emotional health is perceived to be a personal quality that is necessary for appropriate social interactions.

Another emotions-based interpretation of what it means to be social competent is a student's ability to emotionally adapt to diverse situations (Haggerty, Sherrod, Garmezy, & Rutter, 1994). From this perspective, a socially competent individual is able to keep his or her emotions under control, regardless of the current situation. For example, within this framework, being social competent is having the capacity for keeping calm throughout a perceived stressful event. Similarly, emotional intelligence, which allows a student to remain emotionally stable during the ups and downs of a typical school day, reflects that individual's level of social competence (Márquez, Martín, & Brackett, 2006). In this regard, a socially competent student is one who controls his or her emotions rather than being controlled by them in everyday school situations (e.g., peer conflicts and difficult assignments).

While classroom teachers may not consider improving emotional stability or emotional regulation as a domain of instruction, it is important to understand the connection between emotional health and social competence. Emotional stability and regulation is paramount for building and maintaining school relationships and thus largely influences an individual's degree of social participation and feelings of attachment to school. A sizable portion of education research connects positive school relationships and socialization with academic achievement (see Roorda, Koomen, Split, & Oort, 2011, for a meta-analysis of the school achievement effects of positive and negative student–teacher relationships). For peer–peer relationships and the link to academic performance, see Molloy, Gest, and Rulison (2011) and Murray-Harvey (2010). In later chapters, we highlight school- and classwide interventions well suited to collaboration with other service providers, such as school psychologists, that target students' growth in their socioemotional competence. Table 2.3 provides a visual outline of common socioemotional competence frameworks.

Social Competence as a Psychological Construct

Some components of social competence can be categorized as psychological characteristics. For example, students' awareness and subsequent rejection of harmful conduct and unsafe behavior are competencies that greatly influence prosocial behaviors (Bandura, 1999; Bandura, Barbaranelli, Caparara, & Pastorelli, 1996; Caprara et al., 2000). From this perspective, social competence includes the skills students use to consciously disassociate themselves from peers who may engage in inappropriate or dangerous behaviors

TABLE 2.3. Emotional Components of Students' Social Competence

For further reference	Components
Elias & Haynes (2008); Saarni (1999, 2007); Seifer et al. (2004)	Emotional regulation and awareness
Haggerty et al. (1994)	Life skills related to adaptation to diverse situations
Márquez et al. (2006)	Emotional intelligence and stability

(e.g., bullying, stealing, fighting), which predict negative consequences and outcomes (e.g., poor school achievement, delinquency).

At the other end of the spectrum, motivation and persistence are personal psychological characteristics indicative of social competence, in that these character traits permit students to follow through with school commitments (Birch & Ladd, 1996; McClelland, Acock, & Morrison, 2006; Shonkoff & Phillips, 2000; Wentzel, 1999). Also within a psychological framework, social competence can include students' self-direction and self-confidence in personal conduct (see Birch & Ladd, 1996). These internal traits allow individuals to become self-assured, which is typically required for meeting many of the social and academic expectations placed upon them in classroom environments. For example, students with self-direction are often able to work independently and stay on task during potentially distractible situations, both of which are necessary skills for classroom successes.

Goal setting and goal attainment, skills with which many students have difficulty, are also psychological components of social competence. These also happen to be skills that students with disabilities, particularly those with learning disabilities and attention-deficit hyperactivity disorder (ADHD), often find especially challenging. In this view of social competence, setting personal goals that are relevant and appropriate given students' current context and the ensuing use of socially approved methods of satisfying those goals are part of the process of becoming perceived as socially competent. Furthermore, realizing the positive personal and emotional growth that may result from the goal-setting and goal attainment process is indicative of an individual's social maturity, which is an independent interpretation of social competence itself (see Ford, 1992). From this point of view, social competence is a necessary quality for academic achievement, since successful school performance often hinges on one's capacity to accomplish academic goals. We provide descriptions of strategies and curricula aimed at promoting goal-setting and goal attainment skills within both class- and schoolwide approaches in Chapters 3 and 4.

Another important psychological characteristic of social competence is one's ability to adapt to school settings (Henricsson & Rydell, 2006; Howes, 2000; Ladd, 1999; Pianta, Steinberg, & Rollins, 1995). By successfully adjusting to classroom environments, students are thought to be socially competent, since adjustment to an environment helps individuals focus on learning rather than any discomfort from that setting. In a meta-analysis of the social competence of students with disabilities, Nowicki (2003) reports that social competence may be a reflection of individuals' self-perception of the ways in which they fit into the social environment and the ways their participation is received and recognized by others. Thus, social competence can be thought of as a characteristic that depends on exchanges with peers and teachers. We discussed this phenomenon—how perception is critical for social inclusion—in Chapter 1 as one of the specific pathways through which social competence impacts academic achievement.

It is imperative for educators to understand the mechanisms of self-worth and social popularity and the ways in which consequences of both influence school performance. In regard to students with disabilities, these qualities are often impaired; therefore, teachers in inclusive classrooms must be especially mindful of strategies aimed at increasing these skills, for all students regardless of initial ability level, so that each individual in

TABLE 2.4. Psychological Components of Students' Social Competence

For further reference	Components
Bandura (1999); Bandura et al. (1996); Caprara et al. (2000)	Awareness and regulation of harmful conduct and unsafe behavior
Birch & Ladd (1996); McClelland et al. (2006); Shonkoff & Phillips (2000); Wentzel (1999)	Level of personal motivation and persistence
Birch & Ladd (1996)	Self-direction and self-confidence
Ford (1982, 1987, 1992)	Goal setting and attainment
Henricsson & Rydell (2006); Howes (2000); Ladd (1999); Pianta et al. (1995)	Adapting to school environment
Newman (2000); Wentzel et al. (1991); Wentzel (1991)	Feelings of being supported and trusted as well as supporting and trusting others
Nowicki (2003)	Interaction between child's self-perception of social participation and the way this participation is recognized by others
Wentzel (1991)	Self-regulation
Zsolnai (2002)	External and internal control

the classroom can access all the benefits of being perceived as socially competent. See Table 2.4 for characteristics of social competence within psychological frameworks.

Social Competence as Social Skills

In Chapter 1, we introduced social competence as a form of "social knowledge," or the mastery of a constellation of specific behaviors that allow students to meet social norms and expectations (Ames & Ames, 1984; Ford, 1985; Ford, Wentzel, Wood, Stevens, & Siesfeld, 1989; Hartup, 1983; Maccoby & Martin, 1983; Sameroff & Fiese, 2000; Strauss & Quinn, 1997; Wentzel, 1991; Wertsch, 1988). From this point of view, social competence can be interpreted as a confluence of behaviors valued, requested, and expected by classroom teachers that fit into what is considered normal behavior in the school setting (e.g., listening when others are talking, exhibiting patience, cooperation with peers). As we described in Chapter 1, research and practice in education and psychology indicate that, over time, classroom teachers tend to value a particular subset of social skills, such as those social behaviors that enable learning to take priority rather than managing behavior.

Framing social competence as a set of particular social skills is a common approach in elementary school settings. Basic classroom skills, such as listening when others are talking, taking turns with books and other materials, and cooperating during group activities, are valued and expected beginning in the early grades. Social competence from this perspective undergirds the selection and implementation of a wide variety of social skills curricula at the elementary level that target important school-related and teacher-valued competencies. In Chapter 4, we present descriptive information regarding many available social skills curricula that address basic classroom skills often required for adequate school performance.

In an education context, following directions and being able to communicate effectively and appropriately with teachers and peers reflect social competence (Ladd & Burgess, 1999; Rimm-Kaufman, Pianta, & Cox, 2000; Wilson et al., 2007). Effective communication is a component valued by both teachers and peers and is an asset for building and maintaining positive school relationships. At the same time, following directions enables students to work independently and stay on task, which, as previously discussed, is included in some academic-based interpretations of social competence.

Specific to students with learning and behavioral difficulties, researchers (e.g., Ray & Elliott, 2006) have offered social competence as a form of social adjustment. In this interpretation, students' self-concept, their obtained social skills, and the level of support they perceive to be available from teachers and peers can be considered social competencies as they affect social interactions. Thus, supportive agency and positive interactions with teachers and peers are constructs of social competence, which, as independent traits, often predict school success (Curby, Rudasill, Rimm-Kaufman, & Konold, 2008). Together, these competencies reflect students' level of social adjustment. Social adjustment can predict social participation, which, in turn, can predict academic performance, a trajectory presented in Chapter 1 as a pathway through which social competence influences academic achievement.

From a relational perspective, social competence is measured as the quality of relationships an individual develops with teachers and other school staff (Howes, 2000). High-quality relationships between a student and other school agents (e.g., teachers, support staff, peers) increase the motivational level of that student, which is an independent component of social competence and greatly influences academic achievements (see Wentzel, 1998). Research in this area posits that the quality of teacher–student relationships as early as kindergarten can, in fact, predict an individual's social competence—and overall school performance—at the end of elementary school (Howes, 2000). Thus, we can infer that the quality of a student's social relationships can predict social competence, and thus social relationships, in years to come.

It should be noted, however, that simply being "noticed" by peers and teachers is not enough; we cannot confuse nurturing and reciprocal relationships with those resulting from social impact (see Newcomb & Bukowski, 1983, for a reference on social preference and social impact). Social impact is the degree to which students are noticed or recognized as peers; it does not, however, represent friendship. As educators, we need to recognize that it is the positive attributes and overall quality of relationships that determine their level of influence.

In Chapters 3 and 4, we describe effective social skills curricula designed to promote relationship building, along with multiple other personal elements of social competence, at the school- and classwide levels. See Table 2.5 for references of some ways in which social skills are conceptualized as social competence.

TABLE 2.5. Social Components of Students' Social Competence

For further reference	Components
Ames & Ames (1984); Ford (1985); Ford et al. (1989); Hartup (1983); Maccoby & Martin (1983); Sameroff & Fiese (2000); Strauss & Quinn (1997); Wentzel (1991); Wertsch (1988)	Socially responsible behavior, the respect for and behavioral agreement toward social roles and norms
Bursuck & Asher (1986)	"Social knowledge"—knowing what to do and when in school contexts
Caprara et al. (2000)	Prosocial behaviors—helpfulness, sharing, and empathy toward others
Curby et al. (2008)	Engaging in positive interactions with teachers and peers
Gest et al. (2006)	Reputation among peers and teachers
Green et al. (1980)	General acceptance among peers
Ladd & Burgess (1999); Rimm-Kaufman et al. (2000); Wilson et al. (2007)	Ability to communicate effectively with teachers and peers
Howes (2000); Ladd (1990); Wentzel (1991)	Quality of relationships developed and maintained
Newman (1991)	Support/guidance network
Ray & Elliott (2006)	Social adjustment—social skills, self-concept, and perceived support
Wentzel & Caldwell (1997)	Reciprocated friendships and group membership

Social Competence as a Product of Cultural Identity

No discussion of the ways in which social competence can be interpreted is complete without recognizing how cultural and class identity (e.g., race, gender, language proficiency, socioeconomic status) affects students' goals and behaviors in a classroom. We must also recognize how the various aspects of cultural and class identity influence the judgment and values held by adults in schools who are agents in (1) assessing social competence, (2) designing instruction that relies on or influences social competence, and (3) implementing interventions specifically geared to improve social outcomes. As an example of how cultural identity can impact the ways in which social competence can be interpreted, Ferguson (2001) discusses race, specifically the social construction of young black male students, as a significant predictor of which students receive teacher approval—and the associated benefits—in schools and for what behaviors.

Teacher approval is typically understood as the ways in which individual specific students are regarded and perceived by adults in a school setting. Thus, using social competence as an example, social competence is a construct conceptualized and bestowed upon students by those in authoritative positions to approve or disapprove of students and their actions. Using Ferguson's (2001) analysis of the "naughty by nature" composition of young black male students, we can infer that the actions of some students in school settings are interpreted differently than the same actions when exhibited by others.

For example, aggressive behavior is one such action that Ferguson describes as having different interpretations depending on the characteristics of who is displaying it. When enacted by white male students, aggression may be viewed as behavior that results from "boys being boys." However, for black male students, aggression is, at times, viewed as deviant and purposeful rule breaking (Ferguson, 2001). Thus, in Ferguson's (2001) example, acts of aggression by some students are viewed as normal behaviors or as adhering to social expectations for that age group—a conceptualization of social competence. At the same time, acts of aggression from other students are viewed as antisocial—a characteristic of individuals thought to lack social competence.

In a social competence framework, Ferguson may argue that individual teachers define and assess social competence based on social perceptions or biases rather than solely on actual student characteristics or behaviors. In her work, she describes the experiences of students perceived to be of lower status because of cultural identity and thus deemed less socially competent and subsequently denied the benefits associated with being viewed as socially competent.

In a disability context, the ways in which teachers behave toward their students with disabilities can influence how those students are perceived and treated by their peers without disabilities. Thus, the teacher attitudes and behaviors toward students with disabilities that are modeled in the classroom impact not only the learning experiences of those students but the extent to which they are able to participate successfully in the social milieu of the classroom (see Cook, Tankersley, Cook, & Landrum, 2000). For example, when teachers treat students with disabilities as "guests" in an inclusive classroom, these students' peers do so as well; this can close doors to meaningful social interaction opportunities, thereby limiting these students' opportunities to develop and practice social competence among peers (Meyer et al., 1998).

Furthermore, student gender is a variable that impacts teaching styles and thus affects the ways in which certain students are treated in the classroom (Thijs & Verkuyten, 2009). The ways in which teachers behave toward students does have significant bearing on student development of social competence. Thus, it is important for practitioners to keep in mind the impact of gender and its unsuspecting role in students' social competence.

Given the influence of cultural and class identity, discussions of social competence and strategies for enhancing students' social competencies in school settings must recognize the roles that race and other sociocultural variables play in students' lives as well as the impact these variables can have on perceptions of social competence and learner value. Interventions and curricula designed to improve social and emotional behaviors must be sensitive to the influence of others' perceptions. As educators, we should acknowledge the conflicting interpretations of social competence as being located within an individual as opposed to a reflection of the personal values that we bestow upon them.

SUMMARY, CONCLUSION, AND WHAT'S AHEAD

In this chapter, we explored in depth many of the ways in which social competence is constructed and interpreted in school settings. We presented many different elements thought to reflect a student's overall level of social competence, common domains of which include general characteristics and school participation processes and academic, socioemotional, psychological, and basic social skills. It is clear that skills and abilities understood as social competence can be and are interpreted differently in various contexts and through different research or practitioner lenses. A great many interpretations of social competence exist, each with hypothesized and evidenced links to academic achievement. It is important to keep in mind, however, that multiple ways of interpreting or constructing a universally applied term can lead to unclear expectations. For educators interested in promoting social competence in the classroom through methods that will lead to both meaningful short- and long-term outcomes, knowing which areas to focus on is crucial. While the apparent ambiguity and, at times, contradictions in seeking to understand social competence may be dizzying, acknowledging the complexity enhances our ability to promote social competence in thoughtful ways by recognizing assumptions and including context in implementation discussions.

In the remaining chapters of this book, we detail strategies for promoting social competence through the overlapping lenses of academic and emotional competence, psychological well-being, and social skill development. Additionally, in the chapters that follow, we highlight the ways in which various strategies address the social and academic development of students with disabilities. The following list highlights important points from this chapter for leaders to consider when thinking about the role of social competence in inclusive classrooms:

✓ Students with disabilities typically lag behind their peers on many measures of social competence. Therefore, it is important that social competence is addressed early and adequately.

✓ There are many short-term and long-term consequences of high and low levels of social competence, including academic achievement, social participation, personal satisfaction, and employment.

✓ Students who are viewed as socially competent typically perform at higher academic levels and are more likely to meet school-based behavior expectations than peers who are not viewed as socially competent.

✓ Conceptualizations of social competence can be organized into five categories: (1) general characteristics, (2) academic components, (3) socioemotional competence, (4) psychological constructs, and (5) social skills.

✓ Although prosocial behavior is certainly a prime factor in defining social competence, many nonsocial internal behaviors (e.g., staying on task or emotional regulation), which may facilitate socialization, fall under the social competence umbrella.

✓ Awareness of the various ways that social competence is understood and interpreted in school settings enables educators to then consider the many possible ways that social competence can be promoted in the classroom.

✓ Cultural identity influences students' goals and behaviors in the classroom as well as others' perceptions of social competence.

✓ Teacher approval can greatly impact the ways in which students are received by peers and can thus play a significant role in some students' social participation and subsequent academic achievements.

✓ The ways in which teachers treat students with disabilities influences how those students' peers do as well.

CHAPTER 3

Schoolwide Approaches
to Social Skills Development

with CATHERINE R. LARK

The focus of this chapter is to present programs that can be used at the schoolwide (implemented throughout a single school) or districtwide (implemented in multiple elementary schools within a single school district) level to promote the development of social competence for all students. This chapter presents six examples of evidence-based programs that schools or school districts can use to actively promote social competence in the elementary grades, including programs with both promising and strong support. Evidence-based support should be evaluated in terms of both quality and quantity. In order to be classified as having strong support, a program must be backed by (1) quality research, which is defined as well-designed and effectively implemented randomized control design studies, and (2) quantity or number of research studies conducted, which includes two more different school-based implementations of the program and findings that have been replicated by at least one research team in addition to the program developers. Promising support is defined as programs where the evidence supporting the quality of the research does not meet the criteria for strong support yet still provides some support for program effectiveness, and where there are fewer implementations of a program or the research has only been done by a single group of researchers (not independent replications). These definitions for strong and promising support are based on the guidelines suggested in the U.S. Department of Education's (2004) guide, *Identifying and Implementing Educational Practices Supported by Rigorous Evidence.*

Catherine R. Lark, BA, graduated from Austin College and is currently a doctoral student in Psychology at Louisiana State University.

The programs we chose to include in this section are identified as universal or primary prevention programs and have empirical support of both (1) improving student outcomes and (2) implementation effectiveness. The terms *universal prevention* and *primary prevention* are often used interchangeably to describe programs designed to promote social competence at the schoolwide level. In addition, when describing schoolwide programs, the terms *prevention* and *intervention* are also used interchangeably to reflect that a program's goals are to reduce current problems as well as prevent future problems. When evaluating students' outcomes, researchers and practitioners alike need to examine long-term gains. Effective schoolwide programs are the ones that can demonstrate improvements in student outcomes that continue even after children have left the school. The last component, implementation effectiveness, is crucial to evaluating success at the schoolwide level. If the whole school is going to successfully apply a program to improve social competency, there must be effective (1) strategic planning, (2) leadership and development of broad-based program support, and (3) staff development.

Schoolwide programs are often used in conjunction with classroom (Chapter 4) and individual (Chapter 7) programs as part of a three-tiered prevention approach. In a prevention model, schoolwide programs play the role of universal/primary prevention because the strategies are used with all students in a school (both general and special education alike). The classroom-based programs described in Chapter 4 can also serve as primary prevention, in that they are provided to all students in a given classroom. Secondary prevention is the next tier in the prevention continuum. Secondary programs are for students who have some identified risk factor but are not yet experiencing a significant level of problems. Risk factors include a wide variety of issues, from low levels of behavior or academic problems to challenging family dynamics (e.g., parent incarceration or terminal illness). In the area of social competence, risk factors for poor social development can include family conflict, poor social skills, difficulty making friends, and low levels of aggression. Some of the schoolwide and classroom-based programs can be effectively adapted to target the needs of students with identified risks. In addition, some of the individual programs (such as check-in/check-out) are also used at the secondary level. The top tier is known as tertiary prevention. At this level, programs are delivered individually to students who are experiencing serious problems. The programs described in this chapter and in subsequent chapters can be used most effectively when combined to promote the social growth and development of students in special education or who are at risk for referral to special education.

BENEFITS OF SCHOOLWIDE PROGRAMS FOR STUDENTS IN SPECIAL EDUCATION

One question that often arises when using universal schoolwide programs is "How do these programs benefit students in special education when the purpose is to prevent problems before they occur?" In fact, universal programs have a variety of benefits for students in special education, including (1) skill maintenance (the continuing of skill use over time) and generalization (the use of skills in settings outside of the classroom or in settings where those skills were taught), (2) reduction in the number of students needing individualized plans, and (3) the promotion of inclusive practices and an improvement in the overall school climate for all students.

Skill Maintenance and Generalization

Although skill instruction is typically delivered through the same classroom-based format in schoolwide programs, reinforcement of skills occurs across every school environment (e.g., academic and nonacademic classes, hallways, the bus, recess). Additionally, schoolwide programs at the elementary level begin skill development in either PreK or kindergarten and continue to sequentially build skills through fourth or fifth grade (whenever students move on to the next school building). Thus, students are not taught about a skill (e.g., accurately identifying emotions) only one time; instead, they are taught the skill across different grades using different developmentally appropriate activities. Learning social competence skills and receiving feedback on the application of those skills across time and settings promotes the generalization and maintenance of these skills.

Reduction in the Number of Students Needing Individualized Intervention Plans

There is substantial evidence that, when implemented successfully, schoolwide programs can reduce both referrals to special education and the number of students in special education who need individualized behavior plans. For example, Lewis (n.d.) provides an example from a self-contained school where initially 33 students were identified as needing individualized behavioral plans. After the implementation of a schoolwide positive behavior intervention and support process, only five students required individualized intervention plans. While schoolwide programs alone will not address the needs of all students, there is good evidence that they can significantly reduce the number of students who need intensive services. Having fewer students allows teachers more time to dedicate to each student and reduces the overall number of staff required to meet student needs. Finally, when combined with Tier 2 and Tier 3 supports, schoolwide programs are highly effective in providing a foundation for meeting the needs of all students.

Promotion of Inclusion and Improvement of School Climate for Students in Special Education

The development of a more positive school climate and the effective inclusion of students share similar roots. Both are connected to the attitudes and behaviors of school staff toward students with disabilities. Inclusion is promoted in schoolwide programs because all students receive the same instruction and intervention. These programs are not just for students who are experiencing problems; they are for everyone. Additionally, when schools teach and reinforce behaviors related to respect and social competency, students with and without disabilities are more likely to engage in more appropriate behaviors and fewer problem behaviors. When behavior problems are reduced, both students and staff feel safer at school (Bradshaw, Koth, Thornton, & Leaf, 2009). Increases in appropriate behavior and decreases in inappropriate behavior thereby directly connect to the creation of a more positive school climate. In addition to reducing behavior problems, the organizational changes that are possible as a result of successful implementation of schoolwide programs can have a direct and positive effect on school climate (Bradshaw et al., 2009).

CRITERIA FOR SUCCESSFUL SCHOOLWIDE PROGRAMS: WHAT DOES "EVIDENCE BASED" MEAN AT THE SCHOOLWIDE LEVEL?

Collecting evidence for effectiveness at the school level is a challenge of scale. The building of successful schoolwide social competency programs is about more than just one teacher in his or her own classroom deciding to do something differently. Everyone has to do things differently in a similar way. As practitioners are evaluating evidence, they should look to see (1) what outcomes the programs have actually been demonstrated to affect, (2) if the schoolwide curriculum meets the SAFE criteria (Sequenced, Active, Focused, and Explicit), and (3) if there is evidence to show that the program can be implemented effectively in a real-world (school) setting. We have chosen to focus on these three criteria previously used in research (Durlak, Weissberg, Dymnicki, Taylor, & Schellinger, 2011) because we believe they are directly related to evidence of program efficacy and are standards that are most meaningful to practitioners.

Improving Student Outcomes

Evidence-based schoolwide programs that promote social competency are those programs that can demonstrate positive improvements in students' social and emotional skills, behavior, and academic performance. Although academic achievement is not the primary purpose of programs that promote social competency, there is evidence to show that schoolwide programs that promote social and emotional learning can improve academic performance as well (Durlak et al., 2011). Thus, when choosing a program, practitioners should evaluate the evidence of the program's impact on academic performance as well as evidence supporting the program's effectiveness in helping students develop social competence. In doing so, schools will not be forced to choose between social improvement goals and academic improvement goals.

When deciding how to evaluate program outcomes, practitioners should be aware that many schoolwide programs have tools that have been developed and researched alongside the program development and evaluation. Choosing programs that have existing outcome measures can be a benefit for practitioners, because not having to research outcome measures can save time during the program planning process. These tools typically fall into one of two categories: (1) needs assessment tools (related to either school or individual child needs) or (2) outcome measures (e.g., skill development or behavior change). When choosing measures, it is important to make sure that they have good, documented technical properties (i.e., reliability and validity) and that they are the right match for evaluating the outcomes associated with the program you have chosen. This second point is especially critical. Often measures are used because of habit ("These are what we have always used") or for economic factors ("We already have a measure that is similar, so why buy a new one?"). Whatever the reason, if we are not measuring the outcomes that the program is designed to affect or for that matter the outcomes where we want to see improvement, this can lead to flawed decisions. We may incorrectly conclude that a program was not successful when, in fact, it was, but the outcome data did not support this because we measured the wrong thing. Two additional considerations for schools will be the cost of the measures (some assessment tools have to be purchased, while others are free) and the level of skill required to use the tool. Although many programs will provide training on the use of their measures, schools that do not have a staff member with some level of expertise in assessment will need to allocate resources to develop that assessment expertise. Carefully planning for both a preimplementation needs assessment and pre–post outcomes assessment provides schools with a foundation for effective data-based decision making. Good measurement allows schools to accurately and objectively evaluate the strength of the program being implemented in their school.

Following are examples of measures associated with two different programs: Second Step and schoolwide positive behavioral interventions and supports (SWPBIS). The Second Step program has the Devereux Early Childhood Assessment (DECA) (for PreK–K ages), which assesses for the presence of risk and protective factors (one of the goals of the program is to reduce risk factors and increase protective factors), and the Devereux Student Strengths Assessment (DESSA) (for K–5), a behavior rating tool that measures socioemotional competence, resilience, and academic competence. The Second Step measures can be used as both needs assessment (i.e., What risk and protective factors exist in our school?) and progress-monitoring tools (i.e., Has our implementation of the program been successful at reducing risk factors and increasing protective factors?). These tools were developed with the program and are available for purchase from the program publisher.

The SWPBIS researchers have developed a variety of planning/needs assessment tools as well as easy-to-use outcome measures. For example, the School-Wide Evaluation Tool (SET) was developed to be used as part of a school's needs assessment, and the Team Implementation Checklist was developed to assist in strategic planning and evaluation of program implementation. Many of the SWPBIS measures were developed using federal research funds and, as a result, are available for free download from *www.pbis.org*. Finally, just because a measure is associated with one program (i.e., the DESSA was developed by Second Step) does not mean that it cannot be used to measure the outcomes of another program. Practitioners just need to make sure that the measure they choose aligns with the school's desired outcomes and the goals of the program they choose.

Implementation Effectiveness

Successful schoolwide programs begin by developing a team-based strategic planning committee that includes key stakeholders. These stakeholders should be multidisciplinary (including, e.g., administrators, teachers, student support personnel, parents) and representatives of both formal and informal sources of authority within the school. The first job of the team is to conduct a *needs assessment* to identify the school's strengths, weaknesses, and overall needs. The needs assessment begins the data-based decision-making process. The program that is ultimately selected ideally will match the needs identified in this initial assessment. Schoolwide programs are more effective when they are clearly connected with school or district goals (Desimone, 2002). Additionally, schools do not want to spend personnel time and monetary resources "reinventing the wheel." Schools should choose programs that build on their existing strengths. Desimone (2002) also found that the smaller degree of change that was needed, the more likely the change was to be successful.

Once a needs assessment has been completed, the next step is to find an evidence-based approach that meets the identified needs. Certainly, schools can identify a person on the planning team to conduct a literature search to find a well-matching evidence-based program; however, many school personnel have neither the journal database access nor the time to conduct a thorough literature review. Therefore, practitioners may want to start with one of the many emerging databases containing independent reviews of available programs, including the quantity and quality of evidence supporting them. When using these databases, it is important for practitioners to realize that each group has slightly different standards for what they consider "evidence based" as well as a different focus in terms of program content (e.g., a U.S. Department of Education database vs. a Department of Justice database). Thus, if a program of interest is not listed in one database, this does not automatically mean that it is not a quality program. When searching for evidence-based programs, best practice involves searching in multiple locations. See Appendix 3.1 at the end of the chapter for a list of online databases that provide a summary of the quality of evidence available for different intervention programs.

One common source of debate surrounding evidence-based practice is fidelity versus adaptability. (For more information, see Children's Services Council of Palm Beach County's [2007] *Reviewing Research*). Fidelity is about implementing a program as it was designed, and adaptability is about being able to change a program to meet the unique needs of an individual school. As schools choose a schoolwide intervention, it is important for them to investigate whether a program can be altered without affecting the strength of its effectiveness. More specifically, good evidence-based programs will identify which components are critical and, therefore, must be implemented for the program to be effective at increasing social competence and which are optional and can be omitted or changed to tailor the program to the individual needs of a district or individual school.

For example, in the SWPBIS process, it is necessary for a school to develop three to five positively stated global expectations for appropriate school behavior. If this step of developing expectations is left out of the process, it is unlikely that the school will see the positive outcomes demonstrated in research. On the other hand, exactly what those three to five expectations are can vary between schools without negatively affecting outcomes. This option for individualization allows each school to choose different expectations that reflect local norms, values, and language, which, in turn, promotes ownership and buy-in among stakeholder groups. To implement evidence-based programs successfully, practitioners need to clearly identify critical versus optional components. Once critical components have been identified, schools know what they need to implement in order to maintain program efficacy. When optional components are identified, schools know what can be changed to promote acceptability of the program by adapting these components to the individual needs or culture of the school.

Quality professional development is the next critical component in effective implementation. In order for any new program to be implemented successfully, school staff must be provided with high-quality training and feedback. Smith et al. (1997, 1998) and others have found that a relationship exists between weak program implementation and inadequate training. For schoolwide programs, off-site train-the-trainer models are not typically sufficient to support successful implementation. In such models, a group of practitioners will go off-site to learn about the program and then return to the school as the local trainers. Although this is a good model for many school-based activities, it does not work well for schoolwide programming efforts that have multiple components that must be mastered by the trainees (e.g., change process, curriculum components, teaching activities, outcome evaluation) before they are competent to train others. Rather than train-the-trainer programs, practitioners should look for programs that offer on-site training for the whole school. High-quality professional development for successful program implementation has three components: (1) initial training, (2) distributed practice (additional training opportunities or activities that are provided over time), and (3) follow-up consultation and problem solving. The implementation of a successful schoolwide program is grounded in the collaborative consultation model, where the program developers serve as consultants who have expertise in their program and school personnel are the consultees who have expertise in areas such as teaching as well as knowledge of their school.

Leadership and support for the effective implementation of schoolwide programs need to come from both formal and informal sources. Formal sources include more traditional positions of leadership (i.e., superintendent, district administrators, principals) and sources of support (i.e., district- and school-level resources allocated to pay for program materials and training). One important function for these formal roles is the development of a long-term vision for the program. Schoolwide change is not a short-term endeavor; typically, there is an initial implementation process of 3–5 years before a full, multicomponent program is running both effectively and smoothly. This 3- to 5-year time frame includes (1) planning (good programs include preparation and buy-in phases); (2) initial training and running of the program, problem solving, and debugging of the implementation process (e.g., determining the best way to incorporate the program curriculum into the school day or finding the most efficient and effective methods for monitoring student outcomes); and (3) incorporating additional components (such as a parent involvement program or a student steering team to increase student ownership of the program). Finally, formal leaders need to think about how to continue the program past that 3- 5-year initial start-up phase and preserve its effectiveness even when formal leaders change; it is tremendously disheartening for teachers to invest their time and passion into learning and implementing a new, successful program only to see the gains disappear when a new principal or superintendent arrives wanting to implement his or her own program.

Successful implementation of a schoolwide program also requires support and leadership from informal sources. Teachers and other school staff are the ones who will have to execute the program; therefore, schoolwide change cannot be solely a top-down endeavor. In fact, evidence shows that top-down pressure increases the likelihood that school staff will resist program implementation (Smith et al., 1997). One method for reducing top-down pressure is to include in the planning and decision-making processes school staff members who have no formal authority but are highly respected within the school. Every school has personnel who have no formal power but who can influence their peers in either positive or negative ways. In order for implementation to be successful, informal leaders have to be included to maximize their positive influence. Additionally, these informal leaders can serve as models during the implementation process.

While involvement of informal leaders in schoolwide programming is useful, it is not sufficient to ensure success. Two other key components are the development of broad-based support for the program and open communication about program components and goals. Developing buy-in across the majority of school staff is necessary for successful implementation. Research on schoolwide reform has identified a standard of 80% buy-in (meaning that four out of five school staff must voluntarily choose to accept the program) as being necessary before any school-level change is implemented (Desimone, 2002). Allowing a yes–no vote on the program is one technique that is commonly used to measure buy-in. If 80% vote yes, then the school can move ahead with implementation. If the result is a less than 80% favorable vote, the school should put program implementation on hold in order to allow enough time to increase support for the program. Too often schools will push a program through as a top-down mandate and then wonder why it fails. Teachers are professionals and need to be treated respectfully. If they are voting no on something, then they should be viewed as having real concerns that need to be addressed (rather than the standard default of being against change or lazy or, worse yet, not caring about kids). In the case of a no vote, both formal and informal leaders need to spend more time disseminating information and answering questions before moving ahead with implementation. Open dialogue about the program, why it was chosen, and how it will help achieve school goals is also necessary for success. School staff members are more likely to agree to a proposed program if they understand its purpose and demands. Additionally, programs are more successful when staff hold realistic expectations for outcomes and understand clearly how the program will meet school needs. Finally, what teachers believe about the program does matter. Researchers have found that the more closely teacher beliefs match up with program ideals, the less likely they are to resist program implementation (Datnow & Castellano, 2000).

Even if all of the components for effective implementation described in this section are done well, barriers to program success can still arise. Common barriers for successful schoolwide programs are similar to those that arise when promoting inclusion or collaboration and typically fall into one of four categories: professional, pragmatic, attitudinal, and conceptual (Phillips & McCullough, 1990). A common professional barrier that teachers report is not being trained in a particular discipline. When implementing a schoolwide program that promotes social competence, many school staff may perceive a professional barrier. Teacher training typically focuses on how to teach academics, not social interactions. Pragmatic barriers to implementation often occur at the school level and are related to lack of adequate financial or structural support for program implementation. Attitudinal barriers relate to individual beliefs. Some school staff may not believe that increasing social competency is part of the school's mission. When staff have attitudinal barriers, they are more likely to resist program implementation or not implement the program with fidelity. Finally, conceptual barriers typically reflect the culture of the school. Conceptual barriers arise related to role definition and entrenchment problems. When initiating a universal program, schools will have to confront questions about the role of administrators, teachers (both general and special education), other school staff members, parents, and even students in the implementation process. The successful implementation of schoolwide program typically requires everyone from the principal and secretarial staff to teachers and bus drivers to step out of traditional roles and work with kids differently.

A final potential barrier to successful implementation is resistance to change. In schoolwide improvement efforts, teachers and other school personnel are being asked to change, and with change comes resistance. The following are recommendations for addressing resistance in the schoolwide change process:

- *Resistance ≠ problem teacher.* Staff members who exhibit resistance should not be viewed as lazy or as "problems." Often, teachers who exhibit resistance have real concerns (see below for types of resistance).

- *Resistance is normal.* It should be viewed as a normal part of the change process rather than an indicator that staff members are unable or unwilling to do what is being asked of them. Schools are continuous change organizations; every year teachers are faced with the prospect of something new. It can be difficult for them to know whether this is a program that will be around for awhile and, therefore, is worth the investment of time and energy to learn.

- *Be prepared to confront resistance.* Successful programs have a proactive plan in place to identify and address resistance as it arises.

- *Know the different types of resistance and how to address them.* Resistance can come from a variety of different sources, such as anxiety, desire for the status quo, helplessness, defensiveness, lack of understanding, and lack of self-efficacy (Dougherty & Dougherty, 1991).

- *Identify whether resistance is related to a skill, performance, or resource deficit.* Administrators should ask: "Do teachers know what they are supposed to so?" "Do teachers have the support they need to actually implement the program [time and resources] and feel confident in their ability to do so successfully [self-efficacy]?"

- *Acknowledge that change is difficult and communicate real empathy.* Leaders need to first convey to staff that they are aware they are asking staff to do something that is new, time consuming, and for many, at least initially, challenging. Empathy can help leaders to communicate that they understand that schoolwide change requires the time and energy of many people in order to be successful.

- *Respond to the reason behind the resistance.* Leaders should respond to reason behind the resistance rather than directly address problem behaviors. It is easy to criticize staff members who are doing things wrong or to punish people who fail to complete tasks, but such punitive actions will not facilitate staff moving beyond the feelings and behaviors related to resistance, and if anything will entrench the resistance deeper. When students engage in program behaviors, we ask: "What is the function of the behavior?" We have to ask the same type of question for staff members who are not correctly implementing the program: "What are they trying to tell us?" Only by identifying the sources of resistance can we develop an effective intervention to reduce or overcome it.

METHODOLOGY FOR INCLUDING SCHOOLWIDE PROGRAMS

Programs are included in this chapter based on the availability of (1) either strong or promising evidence for improved student outcomes and (2) the existence of information related to implementation effectiveness (e.g., team building, training/professional development, needs assessment, strategic planning). Programs included in this section were also evaluated for evidence of meeting the SAFE criteria, meaning they (1) demonstrate evidence of Sequentially organized activities, (2) utilize Active forms of learning, (3) Focus in some part on promoting social competence, and (4) Explicitly target specific socioemotional development skills (Durlak et al., 2011). See Table 3.1.

Fast Track Program

Authors: Karen L. Bierman, PhD, John D. Coie, PhD, Kenneth A. Dodge, PhD, Mark T. Greenberg, PhD, John E. Lochman, PhD, Robert J. McMahon, PhD, and Ellen E. Pinderhughes, PhD

Publication Date: n.d.

Publisher: Conduct Problems Preventions Research Group

Website: *www.fasttrackproject.org*

Fast Track is a multicomponent program (schoolwide classroom-based social skills instruction, individual child interventions, and family training) with both elementary and adolescent options. Fast Track combines a universal intervention with several individualized interventions targeted at students identified as being at risk for conduct problems (Kusché & Greenberg, 1994). Although this program is not a solely schoolwide universal intervention, we choose to include it as an example of how a Tier 1 (universal) program can be combined with Tier 2 (targeted) interventions.

Fast Track uses the PATHS curriculum (see next program for a complete description) as its universal component and provides child and family interventions for children identified as being at risk for developing conduct disorders (Conduct Problems Prevention Research Group, 2007). The child components include social skill training groups (Friendship Groups); tutoring in reading; and friendship enhancement in the classroom (Peer Pairing). The family components include parent training (to promote

TABLE 3.1. Effective Schoolwide Social Skills Programs

Title	Author	Publisher	Date	Structure and targeted skills	Website
Fast Track	Karen L. Bierman, John D. Coie, Kenneth A. Dodge, Mark T. Greenberg, John E. Lochman, Robert J. McMahon, and Ellen E. Pinderhughes	Conduct Problems Preventions Research Group	n.d.	Fast Track is a multicomponent program (schoolwide classroom-based social skills instruction, individual child interventions, and family training) with both elementary and adolescent options. The child components include social skill training groups, tutoring in reading, and friendship enhancement in the classroom. The family components include parent training (promoting positive family–school relationships) and home visits (to promote the parent's development of problem-solving skills, self-efficacy, and life management skills).	*www.fasttrackproject.org*
Promoting Alternative THinking Strategies (PATHS)	Mark T. Greenberg, Carol A. Kusché, Celene Domitrovich, and Rebecca C. Cortes	Channing Bete Company	1980, 2011, 2012	PATHS is divided by grade level into modules that contain sequentially based units that are designed to build five skill areas: self-control, emotional understanding, positive self-esteem, peer relationships, and interpersonal problem-solving skills. There is a companion family program.	*www.pathstraining.com/main*
Resolving Conflict Creatively Program (RCCP)	Educators for Social Responsibility	Educators for Social Responsibility	1985, 2007	The main objectives of RCCP are reducing violent behavior, promoting care and cooperation among the students, teaching conflict-resolution skills and acceptance of diversity, and promoting a positive school climate. Grade-based lessons are organized into units based on specific core skills such as countering bias, resolving conflicts, fostering cooperation, appreciating diversity, communicating clearly and listening carefully, and expressing feelings and dealing with anger.	*http://esrnational.org/professional-services/elementary-school/prevention/resolving-conflict-creatively-program-rccp*
Responsive Classroom Approach (RCA)	Northeast Foundation for Children, Inc.	Northeast Foundation for Children, Inc.	1981	The RCA consists of five primary schoolwide practices designed to establish and maintain a sense of community, including aligning all school policies and procedures with the program ideals to ensure students receive a consistent message, allocating sufficient resources, having community-bonding activities, involving parents and community members, and organizing the physical environment to promote learning. The program includes 6 core components: morning meetings, rules and logical	*www.responsiveclassroom.org*

Program	Author	Year	Description	Website
			consequences, guided discovery, classroom organization, academic choice, and working with families.	*www.cfchildren.org*
Second Step: Skills for Social and Academic Success (SS)	Committee for Children	1989	The SS schoolwide program is divided into three age groups (Early Learning, Elementary School, and Middle School) with each grade-level sequentially building upon previously learned skills in developmentally appropriate ways. The skills identified are as follows: paying attention, listening, being assertive, ignoring distractions, staying on task, getting along with others, emotional regulation, cooperation, problem solving.	
Schoolwide positive behavioral interventions and supports (SWPBIS)	Multiple	n.d.	SWPBIS uses data-based decision making and outcome evaluation and effective practices designed to improve both student and staff behavior to implement a continuum of evidence-based behavioral and academic interventions. There are four universal elements that all schools have to develop: a clearly defined set of behavioral expectations, a schoolwide process for teaching those expectations, a rewards system for reinforcing students when they exhibit behaviors consistent with school expectations, and a continuum of evidence-based interventions (for both behavior and academic programs).	*www.pbis.org*
	For more information on SWPBIS resources, see Office of Special Education Programs (OSEP) Center on Positive Behavioral Interventions and Supports			
Project ACHIEVE	Howard M. Knoff	1990	Multicomponent program (ages 3–18) includes strategic planning and organizational analysis/development; problem solving, response to intervention, teaming, and consultation processes; effective school, schooling, and professional development; academic instruction linked to academic assessment, intervention, and achievement; PBIS, encompassing social skills instruction linked to behavioral assessment, intervention, and self-management; parent and community training, support, and outreach; data management, evaluation, and accountability. Specific skills targeted include interpersonal, problem solving, conflict resolution, listening, ignoring distractions, accepting consequences, setting goals, handling peer pressure.	*www.projectachieve.info*

the development of positive family–school relationships and to teach the use of effective behavior management skills at home) and home visits (to promote parents' development of problem-solving skills, self-efficacy, and life management skills). The program is designed to be delivered to students in grades 1–5 (with an adolescent component for students in grades 6–10). For elementary school children, the intervention emphasizes understanding and talking about emotions as well as developing self-control and problem-solving skills (Conduct Problems Prevention Research Group, 2007).

At this stage, the program is primarily being implemented at partner research sites, so there is no information available on training or specific program planning or implementation support provided to schools. On the Fast Track website, the developers provide a great deal of information on program data and data collection tools. There are many child- and parent-oriented data collection tools available. Measures that were developed by the research team are available for use at no cost for schools that choose to implement the program and depending on how they are being used are available for no cost to non-Fast Track schools as well. Other measures listed on their website are published instruments and must be purchased from the publisher. The measurement tools resource list is one of the program's strengths, because it allows schools to choose a measure that best matches the specific outcomes that are relevant to their school's goals. Implementation integrity and needs assessment tools are not identified on the website, but in published research differences between schools that are strong implementers versus other schools are discussed (indicating that implementation monitoring tools may be available).

Research on Fast Track has been ongoing since the early 1990s. Initial studies were designed with a longitudinal focus, meaning that they planned from the beginning to follow students in the program into adulthood. The students who started as first graders in the 1990s are now in their 20s, with the most recent follow-up evaluating the remaining participants at age 21. At the end of first grade, significant effects were found on peer ratings of aggression, disruptive behavior, and classroom atmosphere. Additionally, moderate positive effects on children's social, emotional, and academic skills were reported (Conduct Problems Prevention Research Group, 1999). At the end of third grade, many of the gains reported at the end of first grade were maintained, although the academic gains seen at first grade dropped off. When measured at the end of third grade, the differences between control and intervention groups in reading scores or language arts and math grades had faded (Conduct Problems Prevention Research Group, 2002). In subsequent follow-up studies, Fast Track was shown to have a moderate impact on reducing juvenile delinquency (Conduct Problems Prevention Research Group, 2010). In the latest follow-up (Conduct Problems Prevention Research Group, 2011), researchers found a continuing reduction in externalizing behaviors for students who initially (first grade) had the most severe behavior ratings. For students who were initially rated as having less severe behavior problems, the results were mixed.

Sample of Evidence Supporting Efficacy

Conduct Problems Prevention Research Group. (2007). Fast Track randomized controlled trial to prevent externalizing psychiatric disorders: Findings from grades 3 to 9. *Journal of the American Academy of Child and Adolescent Psychiatry, 46*(10), 1250–1262.

Conduct Problems Prevention Research Group. (2010a). Fast Track intervention effects on youth arrests and delinquency. *Journal of Experimental Criminology, 6*, 131–157.

Conduct Problems Prevention Research Group. (2010b). The effects of a multi-year universal social-emotional learning program: The role of student and school characteristics. *Journal of Consulting and Clinical Psychology, 78*(2), 156–168.

Conduct Problems Prevention Research Group. (2011). The effects of the Fast Track preventive intervention on the development of conduct disorder across childhood. *Child Development, 82*(1), 331–345.

Jones, D. E., Godwin, J., Dodge, K. A., Bierman, K. L., Coie, J. D., Greenberg, M. T., et al. (2010). Impact of the Fast Track Prevention Program on health services use by conduct-problem youth. *Pediatrics, 125*(1), e130–e136.

Slough, N. M., McMahon, R. J., & Conduct Problems Prevention Research Group. (2008). Preventing serious conduct problems in school-age youth: The Fast Track Program. *Cognitive and Behavioral Practice, 15*, 3–17.

Promoting Alternative THinking Strategies (PATHS)

Authors: Mark T. Greenberg, PhD, Carol A. Kusché, PhD, Celene Domitrovich, PhD, and Rebecca C. Cortes, PhD

Publication Date: 1980, 2011, 2012

Publisher: Channing Bete Company

Website: *www.pathstraining.com/main*

The PATHS (**P**romoting **A**lternative **TH**inking **S**trategies) curriculum is an elementary school program (PreK–K and grades 1–5/6) designed to improve children's social and emotional competencies. Specifically, PATHS aims to improve the following five areas of socioemotional learning: (1) self-control, (2) emotional understanding, (3) positive self-esteem, (4) peer relationships, and (5) interpersonal problem-solving skills. The PATHS curriculum is divided by grade level into modules. Each module contains sequentially based units that are designed to build socioemotional skill development. Each module also contains various at-home activities that promote parent–child engagement in the socioemotional development process. The at-home component provides additional reinforcement and generalization of the skills learned at school.

The implementation of PATHS is supported by numerous resources available to teachers, including (1) an initial 2- to 3-day workshop on the basics of the program; (2) basic training manuals; (3) six volumes of lessons (one for each grade component), complete with pictures, diagrams, and scripted lesson plans; and (4) follow-up with professional PATHS consultants as needed. Furthermore, lessons are brief (typically only 30 minutes), so the curriculum is easy for teachers to fit into their normal classroom schedule. No outcomes assessment, needs assessment, or organizational planning tools are described in their program materials, but these may be available upon request. Implementation effectiveness has been evaluated in at least one published research study.

The efficacy of PATHS has been demonstrated across subgroups of children, including children in both regular and special education classes, children who are deaf or hearing impaired, and children from both urban and rural communities (Greenberg, 2012). The beneficial results of PATHS can be divided into two categories based upon whether the results show (1) an increase in positive factors or (2) a decrease in negative outcomes for children. Increased positive outcomes from PATHS curriculum include (1) development of effective problem-solving strategies; (2) decreased use of violent or aggressive solutions; (3) increased understanding and recognition of emotions; (4) increased self-control and frustration tolerance; (5) increased ability to plan ahead and solve complex tasks for both normal children and those with special challenges; (6) increased executive function, cognitive flexibility, and low impulsivity during nonverbal tasks; and (7) improved reading achievement for children who are deaf. Reduced problematic outcomes that occurred after 1 year of intervention include (1) decreased externalizing symptoms such as aggression and disruptive behavior; (2) decreased internalizing symptoms such as anxiety, sadness, and withdrawal; (3) more attention and engagement within the class; (4) decreased levels of peer violence; (5) increased levels of prosocial behavior among peers; and (6) improvement in overall classroom atmosphere.

Sample of Evidence Supporting Efficacy

Domitrovich, C. E., Cortes, R. C., & Greenberg, M. T. (2007). Improving young children's social and emotional competence: A randomized trial of the preschool 'PATHS' curriculum. *Journal of Primary Prevention, 28*, 67–91.

Greenberg, M. (2012). Summary of findings on the PATHS® curriculum. Pennsylvania State University, prepared for Channing-Bete Company. Retrieved March, 14, 2012, from *www.prevention.psu.edu/projects/PATHSFindings.html*.

Greenberg, M. T., Kusché, C. A., Cook, E. T., & Quamma, J. P. (1995). Promoting emotional competence in school-aged children: The effects of the PATHS curriculum. *Development and Psychopathology, 7*, 117–136.

Kam, C. M., Greenberg, M. T., & Kusché, C. A. (2004). Sustained effects of the PATHS curriculum on the social and psychological adjustment of children in special education. *Journal of Emotional and Behavioral Disorders, 12*, 66–78.

Resolving Conflict Creatively Program (RCCP)

Author: Educators for Social Responsibility

Publication Date: 1985, 2007

Publisher: Educators for Social Responsibility

Website: *http://esrnational.org/professional-services/elementary-school/prevention/resolving-conflict-creatively-program-rccp*

The Resolving Conflict Creatively Program (RCCP) is a school-based violence prevention program aimed at students in grades K–8. The main objectives of RCCP are (1) reducing violent behavior, (2) promoting care and cooperation among the students, (3) teaching conflict-resolution skills as well as acceptance of diversity, and (4) promoting a positive school climate. The RCCP approach is based on the principle that aggression is a learned behavior. Therefore, to decrease aggression and violence in schools, school staff should teach and reinforce nonaggressive behaviors, thereby promoting the learning of prosocial skills (rather than aggressive behaviors). RCCP lessons are organized into units based on specific core skills such as countering bias, resolving conflicts, fostering cooperation, appreciating diversity, communicating clearly and listening carefully, and expressing feelings and dealing with anger. Within each lesson, however, the teacher takes a hands-off approach and serves more as a moderator for class discussion rather than an actual lecturer, so as to give the students more active involvement in the program.

RCCP provides many options for training and support. There are training options for everyone from administrators and teachers to bus drivers and ancillary school staff. Before RCCP can be implemented, teachers must first complete 25 hours of training conducted by experienced RCCP staff members. Trainers provide specific instruction on how to teach conflict resolution strategies and promote positive peer relationships. After initial training, teachers implement the RCCP curriculum within their classrooms and receive follow-up support from RCCP staff as needed. In addition to teacher training, RCCP provides other training components and resources, including (1) instruction on how to collect initial data in order to assess the needs of the particular school; (2) a planning meeting to customize the program to meet those particular needs; (3) two volumes of classroom lessons; (4) peer mediation training for school coordinators, adult coaches, and students; (5) administrative training; (6) family workshops so that parents can become involved with the program; and (7) training for any other paraprofessionals such as bus drivers and security staff. Other than conducting a needs assessment, no other assessment options are described.

Researchers evaluating RCCP effectiveness have looked at how the rates of aggressive behavior committed by children who have received RCCP intervention compare with the typical rates of increased aggressive behavior experienced by children during middle childhood. Research has shown that RCCP does significantly reduce the rate at which these violent behaviors normally increase (Aber, Pedersen, Brown, Jones, & Gershof, 2003). Aber, Brown, and Jones (2003) explain that RCCP reduces the rate of violence by decreasing social-cognitive problems (such as hostile attribution bias, or the misperception of another person's behavior as hostile and aimed directly at oneself) as well as behavioral issues (such as conduct problems, depression, and aggressive fantasies). Additionally, the same researchers found that RCCP implementation is related to increases in academic achievement, particularly in math.

Sample of Evidence Supporting Efficacy

Aber, J., Brown, J., & Jones, S. (2003). Developmental trajectories toward violence in middle school childhood: Course, demographic differences, and response to school-based intervention. *Development and Psychology, 39*(2), 324–348.

Aber, J., Pedersen, S., Brown, J., Jones, S., & Gershoff, E. (2003). *Changing children's trajectories of development: Two-year evidence for the effectiveness of a school-based approach to violence prevention.* Columbia University, prepared for the National Center for Child in Poverty. Retrieved March 23, 2012, from *www.nccp.org/publications/pub_554.html.*

DeJong, W. (1993). Building the peace: The Resolving Conflict Creatively Program (RCCP). U.S. Department of Justice, prepared for the National Institute of Justice. Retrieved March 23, 2012 from *www.ncjrs.gov/App/publications/Abstract.aspx?id=149549.*

Lawrence, A. J., Jones, S. M., Brown, J. L., Chaudry, N., & Samples, F. (1998). Resolving conflict creatively: Evaluating the developmental effects of a school-based violence prevention program in neighborhood and classroom context. *Development and Psychopathology, 10,* 187–213.

Selfridge, J. (2004). Resolving Conflict Creatively Program: How we know it works. *Theory into Practice, 43*(1), 59–66.

The Responsive Classroom Approach (RCA)

Author: Northeast Foundation for Children, Inc.

Publication Date: 1981

Publisher: Northeast Foundation for Children, Inc.

Website: *www.responsiveclassroom.org*

The Responsive Classroom Approach (RCA) is a research-based approach to education created by the Northeast Foundation for Children (NEFC). This approach combines both academic and social learning in order to help children grow and thrive academically, emotionally, and socially (Rimm-Kaufman, Fan, Chiu, & You, 2007). The RCA is targeted at elementary school students and involves both classroom and schoolwide components. One of the key components of the program is building a strong sense of community within the school setting, which, in turn, supports the development of positive learning environments for students (Rimm-Kaufman et al., 2007). The RCA consists of five primary schoolwide practices designed to establish and maintain a sense of community: (1) aligning all school policies and procedures with the program ideals to ensure students receive a consistent message across their daily activities; (2) allocating sufficient resources (time, money, space, and personnel) to program implementation; (3) having all-school community-bonding activities that bring students and teachers together; (4) involving parents and other community members in educational activities (such as volunteer work); and (5) organizing the physical environment of the school to promote learning. These community-based strategies end up being beneficial not only for the students but also for the faculty as well. For instance, Rimm-Kaufman and Sawyer (2004) found that in schools where the RCA was implemented, teachers reported increased levels of self-efficacy beliefs and more positive sentiments about the teaching profession.

The core belief of RCA is that both academic and socioemotional skills are equally vital to the optimization of student learning. The program contains six core components that can be used both alone and together to facilitate this combination of social and academic growth (Horsch, Chen, & Nelson, 1999):

1. *Morning meeting.* At the beginning of each school day, the classroom teacher and students come together to greet one another and talk about the upcoming day. Morning meetings foster a sense of community between the students and teacher, provide an opportunity for students to get to know one another better, give students an opportunity to practice and receive feedback on social skills (such as peer interaction, quiet listening, and public speaking), and prepare students for the upcoming day because they now know what to expect.

2. *Rules and logical consequences.* Children are given the opportunity to help establish rules and guidelines for the classroom. This activity encourages open communication and collaboration, thus strengthening the relationship between the teacher and students. Additionally, children have an opportunity to practice problem-solving skills and develop a sense of classroom ownership.

3. *Guided discovery.* Teachers take the time to carefully introduce each learning item or technique before it is used. Children are also given the opportunity to individually explore the materials through open-ended activities. Guided discovery not only teaches children the topic or skill but also fosters a sense of creativity and independence.

4. *Classroom organization.* Teachers organize the classroom to foster interaction, independence, and productive learning. They also use classroom decorations to promote diversity among the students by reflecting the children's various cultures. Students' interests in school can be strengthened by creating a fun and productive environment in which they can learn.

5. *Academic choice.* Children are given the option to choose among several study topics when appropriate. Choice of what to study helps children develop a sense of autonomy and control within the learning process. Furthermore, children are motivated to do better because they are more interested in topics that they choose.

6. *Working with families.* Ongoing communication between school and home is important. With ongoing, open communication, parents are able to provide teachers with insights about their child in order to help promote their child's success within school. At the same time, teachers can also provide parents with feedback on how to encourage their child's social and academic development at home.

As with other schoolwide programs, the developers of RCA identify that a commitment to a multiyear implementation is necessary to achieve optimal student and school improvement outcomes. The first step in the implementation process involves initial teacher training, with a focus on classroom implementation. The second step is to broaden the scope of the implementation to the schoolwide level, with a focus on the five community-building activities described previously. To facilitate effective implementation at each stage, the NEFC provides several resources for ongoing education about RCA, including a combination of 1-day workshops and week-long institutes, where educators see the various components (described in detail shortly) of the approach in action and follow-up consultation that involves on-site lesson demonstrations, individual consultations, and more advanced implementation strategies. Annual conferences are held each summer where administrators and educators come together to discuss their various experiences with RCA. These annual conferences allow schools to build a broad base of support for program implementation. Rather than relying solely on outside consultants or researchers for support, schools can build a network of other practitioners who are facing the same types of real-world implementation successes and challenges. Finally, the NEFC provides various program-related publications, including books, DVDs, posters, and free quarterly newsletters to support ongoing staff and program development.

For an additional cost, schools can purchase the *Responsive Classroom Assessment*. Teachers can use this measure to self-evaluate their own implementation of the program in their classroom. The Responsive Classroom Assessment is a detailed self-assessment questionnaire that gives teachers feedback about how to improve problem areas and allows teachers to collect data in order to track student improvement.

Several researchers have documented positive social and academic gains associated with the RCA. In 1½-year-long study (Elliott, 1995), the impact of RCA on student behavior and evaluated teacher acceptability of the program was investigated. A moderate positive impact was found on student behavior, with the hypothesis that given a longer time period, greater behavior gains would be observed (Elliott, 1995). Teachers rated the program as having a high level of acceptability (i.e., they liked the program, thought it was useful and appropriate for their students and worth the time and resource investment). High acceptability ratings are critical for the success of school-wide programs. The higher acceptability that a program has, the more likely schools are to get an acceptable level of buy-in for the program.

A subsequent 3-year quasi-experimental study was conducted to further investigate the impact of the RCA (Rimm-Kaufman et al., 2007). In this study, three schools that chose to implement RCA were compared with three schools that chose not to implement. The findings were consistent with those from earlier studies (i.e., Elliott, 1995): Children in participating schools had increased academic and social outcomes compared with children in nonparticipating schools. Specifically, they found increases in math and reading scores, improved ratings of social skills, and more positive feelings about school. Additionally, teachers also benefited, reporting that they felt more effective and positive about teaching, were able to offer higher quality instruction, and collaborated more often with colleagues (Rimm-Kaufman et al., 2007). One strength of this study was that researchers were able to replicate earlier findings. The major limitation was the lack of random assignment. Because schools got to choose to participate or not, there could have been some common factor to participating schools compared with nonparticipating schools that contributed to the differences in outcomes. This limitation does not mean that the data are not useful to schools that are considering adopting the program; instead, schools just need to evaluate the outcomes with this limitation in mind. We point out these strengths and limitations to help schools begin thinking about how to evaluate (1) available evidence about program outcomes and (2) different types of research designs.

Sample of Evidence Supporting Efficacy

Elliott, S. N. (1995). *Final evaluation report: The Responsive Classroom Approach: Its effectiveness and acceptability*. Washington, DC: Author.

Elliott, S. N. (1997). *The Responsive Classroom Approach: Its effectiveness and acceptability in promoting social and academic competence.* University of Wisconsin, Madison, prepared for the Northeast Foundation for Children. Retrieved from *www.responsiveclassroom. org/past-research.*

Horsch, P., Chen, J., & Nelson, D. (1999). Rules and rituals: Tools for creating a respectful, caring learning community. *Phi Delta Kappan, 81*(3), 223–227.

Rimm-Kaufman, S. E., Fan, X., Chiu, Y.-J., & You, W. (2007). The contribution of the Responsive Classroom Approach on children's academic achievement: Results from a three year longitudinal study. *Journal of School Psychology, 45,* 401–421.

Rimm-Kaufman, S. E., & Sawyer, B. E. (2004). Primary-grade teachers' self-efficacy beliefs, attitudes toward teaching, and discipline and teaching practice priorities in relation to the "responsive classroom" approach. *Elementary School Journal, 104*(4), 321–341.

Second Step:
Skills for Social and Academic Success (SS)

Author: Committee for Children

Publication Date: 1989, 1991, 1997, 2011

Publisher: Committee for Children

Website: *www.cfchildren.org/second-step.aspx*

Second Step (SS) can be implemented at both the schoolwide and classroom-based levels. For the purpose of Chapter 3, we present information related to the schoolwide application. Information on evidence supporting the classroom-based curriculum is presented in Chapter 4. Second Step is a social skills program developed by the Committee for Children to increase socioemotional competence and decrease both impulsive and aggressive behavior. The target audience for this program runs almost the full continuum of school-age students, from young children in early education programs to early adolescents in middle school (typical ages 4–14 years). Research on SS has demonstrated that the program can be used at the schoolwide level to meet the goals of increasing prosocial behaviors and decreasing problem behaviors. The SS program is grounded in research related to developmentally appropriate practice as well as cognitive, behavioral, and social learning theories. The SS schoolwide program is divided into three age groups (early learning, elementary school, and middle school), with each grade level sequentially building upon previously learned skills in developmentally appropriate ways. The skills identified at each level are as follows:

1. The early learning program for PreK is the newest SS program. It is geared toward increasing young children's school readiness and social success. The two main components at this level are promoting socioemotional competence and teaching self-regulation skills. These components are taught through the following lesson units: (1) skills for learning (listening, focusing attention, self-talk, and being assertive); (2) empathy (recognizing and understanding other people's emotional state or feelings);

(3) emotion management (coping with strong emotions and expressing them in appropriate ways); (4) friendship skills and problem solving; and (5) brain builders (reinforcement of skills in fun and applied activities).

2. The goal of the elementary school (K–5) program is to improve students' school success and reduce problem behaviors. Building on the early learning programs, socioemotional competence and self-regulation are also the central focus at the elementary level. The elementary program even contains some of the same units (listening, empathy, emotion management, problem solving, and brain building), so that students are reexposed to concepts in a developmentally appropriate manner. The elementary program also introduces a new component: risk and protective factors. Classroom units promote protective factors (such as social skills and school connectedness) while reducing risk factors (such as peer rejection, impulsivity, inappropriate classroom behavior, early initiation of problem behavior, and peer rewards for antisocial behavior).

3. The middle school program integrates previously learned skills (empathy and communication, emotion management, and problem solving) in order to protect students from the increasing problems encountered in middle school such as, bullying, cyberbullying, peer pressure, and substance abuse.

The SS program contains several components that support implementation effectiveness. First, the program has a variety of well-designed training activities (including options for online training and facilitator-based models, both of which include video-based modules). In addition, the Committee for Children provides other resources such as recommended websites, free training tips, and books available for purchase. Since the Committee for Children views staff support as key to successful program implementation, booster trainings are also available for purchase. Booster training can help educators (1) assess implementation effectiveness, (2) increase commitment to the program, (3) share effective program strategies and ideas, (4) resolve any implementation problems, and (5) practice such skills as coaching and role-play facilitation. Second, an administrator's guide is available to support integration of SS into the school community as well as the curriculum. Finally, program developers provide schools with information and ideas for conducting evaluations of student outcomes and the implementation process. For example, the DECA and DESSA tools are available for purchase. These tools can be used to evaluate the risk and protective factors that exist in the school environment and to evaluate individual student skills related to social competence.

Evidence for the effectiveness of SS comes from both the design and research phases of the program's development. Researchers began collecting both formative and summative evidence on the SS program while it was being developed. Program designers used a series of research projects to test out different aspects of the SS program (Beland, 1989, 1991; Moore & Beland, 1992). In these initial studies, students showed improvement in their knowledge of social skills and their ability to solve problems as well as a reduction in aggressive behavior. Teachers in the initial studies provided feedback that allowed researchers to refine program content, structure, and implementation. In these initial studies, the teachers rated the program as highly acceptable (i.e., easy to use, fit well within their classroom curriculum, engaging for students). Since the initial development, the Committee for Children has continued to solicit feedback from teachers and collect ongoing research on effectiveness of both instructional practices and skill development. All of that data were used to design updated versions of the elementary and early learning programs that were released in 2012. This new version continues to be teacher friendly and its lesson examples, scenarios, and videos have been modernized to reflect the experiences of current students.

Other research evaluating SS focused solely on program outcomes. Grossman et al. (1997) conducted a randomized control design study in which 12 schools were assigned to either participate in SS or serve as a no-treatment control group. Researchers found that SS had the strongest impact on reducing aggressive behaviors (in both classroom and nonclassroom settings); other behaviors such as problem-solving and social skills use had more mixed results. It is possible that the study did not last long enough to be able to adequately evaluate gains in areas other than aggression. Other studies (e.g., Cooke et al., 2007) have found that students who participated in SS show significant improvements in prosocial skills (i.e., caring, cooperation, consideration of others), increases in coping skills, and reductions in aggression. In addition, Cooke et al. (2007) found continuing evidence of high levels of teacher acceptability and teacher confidence in the effectiveness of the program at helping their students.

Sample of Evidence Supporting Efficacy

Beland, K. (1989). *Second Step, grades 4–5: Summary report.* Seattle, WA: Committee for Children.

Beland, K. (1991). *Second Step, preschool–kindergarten: Summary report.* Seattle, WA: Committee for Children.

Cooke, M. B., Ford, J., Levine, J., Bourke, C., Newell, L., & Lapidus, G. (2007). The effects of city-wide implementation of "Second Step" on elementary school students' prosocial and aggressive behaviors. *Journal of Primary Prevention, 28*(2), 93–115.

Edwards, D., Hunt, M. H., Meyers, J., Grogg, K. R., & Jarrett, O. (2005). Acceptability and student outcomes of a violence prevention curriculum. *Journal of Primary Prevention, 26*, 401–418.

Frey, K. S., Hirschstein, M. K., & Guzzo, B. (2000). Preventing aggression by promoting social competence. *Journal of Emotional and Behavioral Disorders, 8*, 102–112.

Frey, K. S., Nolen, S. B., Edstrom, L. V., & Hirschstein, M. K. (2005). Effects of a school-based social-emotional competence program: Linking children's goals, attributions, and behavior. *Journal of Applied Developmental Psychology, 26*, 171–200.

Grossman, D. C., Neckerman, H. J., Koepsell, T. D., Liu, P. Y., Asher, K. N., Beland, K., et al. (1997). Effectiveness of a violence prevention curriculum among children in elementary school: A randomized control trial. *Journal of the American Medical Association, 277*, 1605–1611.

Moore, B., & Beland, K. (1992). *Evaluation of Second Step, preschool–kindergarten: A violence prevention curriculum kit. Summary report.* Seattle, WA: Committee for Children.

Taub, J. (2002). Evaluation of the Second Step violence prevention program at a rural elementary school. *School Psychology Review, 31*(2), 186–200.

Schoolwide Positive Behavioral Interventions and Supports (SWPBIS)

Author and Publisher Information: None; for more information on SWPBIS resources see Office of Special Education Programs (OSEP) Center on Positive Behavioral Interventions and Supports

Website: *www.pbis.org*

Schoolwide positive behavioral interventions and supports (SWPBIS) is different from the first four programs described previously in that it is specifically characterized as *not* being an intervention, curriculum, or program. Instead, it is a systems-based process that uses (1) data-based decision making and outcome evaluation and (2) effective practices designed to improve both student and staff behavior to implement a continuum of evidence-based behavioral and academic interventions. SWPBIS is grounded in behavior and social learning theories. In the SWPBIS process, there are four universal elements that all schools have to develop: (1) a clearly defined set of behavioral expectations, (2) a schoolwide process for teaching those expectations, (3) a rewards system for reinforcing students when they exhibit behaviors consistent with school expectations, and (4) a continuum of evidence-based interventions (for both behavior and academic programs). While the SWPBIS process alone has demonstrated effectiveness at improving behavioral, social, and academic outcomes as well as the social climate of a school, it is often combined with a specific curriculum (such as one of the schoolwide programs described in Chapter 3 or one of the classroom or individual programs described in Chapters 4 and 5). Combining SWPBIS with a specific curriculum can help schools target their specific needs without having to spend time and resources developing their own program and can allow schools to concurrently develop Tier 1 and Tier 2 programs. The last example in this chapter, Project ACHIEVE, is a program that combines the SWPBIS process with a specific curriculum (Stop & Think, which is described as an evidence-based classroom curriculum in Chapter 4). Finally, positive behavioral interventions and supports (PBIS) is itself not limited to being supported by strong evidence schoolwide (Tier 3) level alone. A great deal of research has been conducted on how a PBIS approach can be effectively utilized at the Tier 2 and Tier 1 levels as well. For more information on PBIS research at all three tiers, see the research page on *www.pbis.org* (*www.pbis.org/research/default.aspx*). For those who are interested in a detailed list of research studies related to each tier, the complete report (*Is School-wide Positive Behavior Support an Evidence-Based Practice?*) is available for download. While its title focuses on SWPBIS, the report covers a wide variety of evidence-based applications for this process.

Because of (1) so many researchers being involved in investigating and implementing SWPBIS, (2) the existence of several research and dissemination centers supported by the U.S. Department of Education, and (3) the fact that SWPBIS itself is a process rather than a program, there are a great number of resources available to schools for implementation and evaluation. The process of SWPBIS includes the development of a school-based team and a plan to screen and monitor students' behaviors and academic achievement, conducting a school-level evaluation of effective strategies and practices, and monitoring to evaluate whether evidence-based practices are being implemented with fidelity (accuracy). Researchers investigating the SWPBIS model have developed a variety of free or low-cost tool that schools can use to evaluate both student outcomes (i.e., School-Wide Information Software [SWIS], a web-based software program for collecting and analyzing office discipline referrals) and implementation activities/effectiveness (i.e., SET; PBIS Leadership Team Assessment Tool; Benchmarks of Quality). Additional tools are available to evaluate secondary (students with specific risk factors) and tertiary (individual) tier programs and to collect feedback from other stakeholders (i.e., parent feedback collected using Family Satisfaction Tool). All of these tools identified as well as others are available at either *www.pbis.org* or *www.swis.org*.

As for training and implementation support, again many resources exist. There are regional support centers, and support is provided by many individual states' Departments of Education. Additional resources for implementation and assessment, including links to other PBIS research centers and to individual state PBIS websites can be found on the *www.pbis.org* links page: *www.pbis.org/links/default.aspx*. In addition to the online resources for SWPBIS, we have included some print-based resources that practitioners may find useful. These are user-friendly books that include many real-world examples, tools, and reproducibles.

Algozzine, B., Daunic, A. P., & Smith, S. W. (2010). *Preventing problem behaviors: School-wide programs and classroom practices* (2nd ed.). Thousand Oaks, CA: Corwin Press.

Crone, D. A., & Horner, R. H. (2003). *Building positive behavior support systems in schools: Functional behavioral assessment.* New York: Guilford Press.

Jackson, L., & Panyan, M. V. (2002). *Positive behavioral support in the classroom: Principles and practices.* Baltimore: Brookes.

Sailor, W., Dunlap, G., Sugai, G., & Horner, R. (Eds.). (2009). *Handbook of positive behavior support (Issues in clinical child psychology series).* New York: Springer.

Stormont, M., Lewis, T., Beckner, R. S., & Johnson, N. W. (Eds.). (2007). *Implementing positive behavior support systems in early childhood and elementary settings.* Thousand Oaks, CA: Corwin Press.

While SWPBIS is a seen as a process rather than a program, researchers have documented the positive effects that using SWPBIS can have on all members of the school community. There is evidence from numerous studies to show that effective implementation of SWPBIS provides benefits not only for students but also for faculty and staff.

- *Student outcomes.* SWPBIS results in decreased rates of teacher-reported bullying and peer rejections compared with schools where SWPBIS was not implemented (Waasdorp, Bradshaw, & Leaf, 2012). Researchers have also found that SWPBIS reduces overall problem behavior, including suspensions, expulsions, and office discipline referrals (Bradshaw, Mitchell, & Leaf, 2010).

- *Academic outcomes.* Since reduced rates of problem behavior means that more time will be spent in the classroom; researchers have also examined the effect of SWPBIS implementation on academic achievement. Lassen, Steele, and Sailor (2006) found that students' reading and math scores on standardized tests were indeed correlated with the number of problem behaviors that occurred in a school. Lassen et al. (2006)

also found that students' math scores increased significantly throughout the 3 years of SWPBIS implementation. The reading scores also increased during the 3 years; however, it was not a statistically significant increase.

- *Effects on academic engagement.* One broader benefit of SWPBIS is that students report that they are more engaged in their educational experience because they perceive school as being a more safe and supportive environment (Sugai & Horner, 2008).

- *Adult outcomes.* SWPBIS can have a positive effect on the adults in a school. Researchers have found that in SWPBIS schools teachers report more positive relationships with colleagues, are able to more directly focus on academics, and view their school as an overall healthier, more positive place to be (Bradshaw et al., 2009).

In a final note, of all the programs reviewed by the authors, SWPBIS has the most consistent findings that have been replicated independently in the largest number of schools. At publication, some form of SWPBIS is being implemented in more than 7,000 schools across the United States (*www.pbis.org*). There are several federally funded national research centers that conduct SWPBIS research and training. These centers are also available to assist schools with the implementation process. Taken together, the replicated positive outcomes, broad availability of implementation support, and the research-based knowledge of systems change (what it takes to enact a successful organizational change process) in our opinion makes SWPBIS a program that all schools should strongly consider.

Sample of Evidence Supporting Efficacy

Bradshaw, C. P., Koth, C. W., Thornton, L. A., & Leaf, P. J. (2009). Altering school climate through school-wide positive behavioral interventions and supports: Findings from a group-randomized effectiveness trial. *Prevention Science, 10*(2), 100–115.

Bradshaw, C. P., Mitchell, M., & Leaf, P. (2010). Examining the effects of school-wide positive behavioral interventions and supports on student outcomes: Results from a randomized controlled effectiveness trial in elementary schools. *Journal of Positive Behavior Interventions, 12*(3), 133–148.

Horner, R., Sugai, G., Smolkowski, K., Todd, A., Nakasato, J., & Esperanza, J., (2009). A randomized, wait-listed control trial of school-wide positive behavior support in elementary schools. *Journal of Positive Behavior Interventions, 11*(3), 133–144.

Lassen, S. R., Steele, M. M., & Sailor, W. (2006). The relationship of school-wide positive behavior support to academic achievement in an urban middle school. *Psychology in the Schools, 43*(6), 701–712.

McIntosh, K., Chard, D., Boland, J., & Horner, R. (2006). A demonstration of combined efforts in school-wide academic and behavioral systems and incidence of reading and behavior challenges in early elementary grades. *Journal of Positive Behavior Interventions, 8*(3), 146–154.

Nelson, J. R. (1996). Designing schools to meet the needs of students who exhibit disruptive behavior. *Journal of Emotional and Behavioral Disorders, 4*, 147–161.

Sugai, G., & Horner, R. H. (2008). What we know and need to know about preventing problem behavior in schools. *Exceptionality, 16*, 67–77.

Waasdorp, T. E., Bradshaw, C. P., & Leaf, P. J. (2012). The impact of school-wide positive behavioral interventions and supports (SWPBIS) on bullying and peer rejection: A randomized controlled effectiveness trial. *Archives of Pediatrics and Adolescent Medicine, 116*(2), 149–156.

Project ACHIEVE

Author: Howard M. Knoff, PhD

Publication Date: 1990

Publisher: Project ACHIEVE

Website: *www.projectachieve.info*

Project ACHIEVE is a universal intervention described as a comprehensive school reform program. The target population spans the education spectrum, covering students from preschool through high school (ages 3–18 years). It is a multicomponent program and includes the following features: (1) strategic planning and organizational analysis/development; (2) problem-solving, response-to-intervention, teaming, and consultation processes; (3) effective school, schooling, and professional development; (4) academic instruction linked to academic assessment, intervention, and achievement; (5) positive behavioral interventions and supports (PBIS), encompassing social skills instruction linked to behavioral assessment, intervention, and self-management; (6) parent and community training, support, and outreach; and (7) data management, evaluation, and accountability.

The Project ACHIEVE program and its components are grounded in social learning theory and the PBIS process. Therefore, much of the program focuses on changing how school staff respond to problem behaviors. There are, however, some specific strategies that are part of Project ACHIEVE. First, social competencies are promoted using the Stop & Think Social Skills Program (described in detail in Chapter 4). Stop & Think utilizes features of social learning theory, such as direct skill instruction, modeling of appropriate behavior, and role-playing or active strategy use so that students can receive direct feedback on their skill performance. Second, schools use the SWPBIS process to develop schoolwide discipline, behavior management, and school safety plans that teach and reinforce expectations for appropriate behavior. Finally, functional behavioral assessment is used to identify effective interventions for students who need more individualized intervention plans than the schoolwide program provides. With this combination of components, Project ACHIEVE can be used to address student needs at Tiers 1 (universal: a schoolwide program), 2 (secondary: targeting students with specific risk factors), and 3 (tertiary: individual student planning).

The components of Project ACHIEVE reflect a focus on the implementation process. To support schools in effective implementation, the author of Project ACHIEVE provides a variety of free needs assessment and strategic planning tools. Additionally, training for program implementation is provided, including in-service training and classroom-based demonstrations as well as technical consultation and follow-up.

A variety of free or low-cost outcome measures are available for schools that use the program.

Outcomes for Project ACHIEVE include improvements for (1) students in behavior, social skills, and academics; (2) staff in their consistency and confidence in responding to discipline issues; and (3) the overall school climate, making the school a more positive place to be. Kilian, Fish, and Maniago (2006) conducted a pre–post assessment of the program as it was being implemented in an elementary school (grades 3–6). The researchers found improvements in prosocial skills, appropriate behavior, and decision making. They also found decreases in disruptions in both classroom and nonclassroom settings, reductions in office disciplinary referrals, and fewer students being suspended. In another study, Knoff and Batsche (1995) looked at how the implementation process utilized by Project ACHIEVE can be used to support school organizational development while improving student outcomes. This was a 4-year study that began with effective planning. The first year of the study was spent developing staff buy-in, conducting prerequisite skills training (that could be built on during later training sessions), providing consultation support regarding implementation strategies, and assisting with decisions relating to data collection. They used a combination of top-down and bottom-up strategic planning activities to increase buy-in and improve the likelihood of a successful implementation. Schools considering adopting a schoolwide program will find the information in the Knoff and Batsche (1995) article useful, because it details all of the planning steps before and during the implementation process. Finally, related to implementation, the authors noted that factors such as creativity, commitment, and understanding are critical to the success of schoolwide program. After the first preplanning year, there were 3 years of data collection. From year 1 to year 3, improvements were seen in both behavior and academics (Knoff & Batsche, 1995). For example:

- *There were fewer students referred to special education.* In the first year, 10% (*N* = 66) of students were referred for testing compared with only 2% (*N* = 16) in year 3. Additionally, the Project ACHIEVE school reported significantly fewer referrals than a comparison school.
- *There were fewer disciplinary referrals in both classroom and nonclassroom settings.* During year 1, total disciplinary referrals were 73 incidents per 100 students compared with 53 incidents per 100 students during year 3.
- *Retention rates decreased.* In year 1, the retention rate was 6% of the school population, whereas during year 3 it was less than 1%.
- *Out-of-school suspensions decreased.*
- *Test scores increased.* Moderate increases were reported in academic achievement (as measured by test scores).

Sample of Evidence Supporting Efficacy

Kilian, J. M., Fish, M. C., & Maniago, E. B. (2006). Making school safe: A system-wide school intervention to increase student prosocial behaviors and enhance school climate. *Journal of Applied School Psychology, 23*(1), 1–30.

Knoff, H. M. (2000). Organizational development and strategic planning for the millennium: A blueprint toward effective school discipline, school safety, and crisis prevention. *Psychology in the Schools, 37*(1), 17–32.

Knoff, H. M., & Batsche, G. M. (1995). Project ACHIEVE: Analyzing a school reform process for at-risk and underachieving students. *School Psychology Review, 24*(4), 579–603.

SUMMARY, CONCLUSION, AND WHAT'S AHEAD

The schoolwide approaches described in this chapter are potential resources for elementary schools that desire to help all students develop social competencies. In a prevention model, universal interventions are just the first layer in a continuum of services that can be provided to improve the outcomes of students both with and without disabilities. Universal components can prevent 80% or more of the academic and behavior problems within a given school (when implemented effectively), often resulting in a reduction in the number of special education referrals. These programs, however, are most effective when combined with targeted or classroom-based programs (Chapter 4) and individualized interventions (Chapter 5) for social skill development. The effectiveness of this multitiered approach is especially true for students with moderate to severe disabilities. The following is a list of points that teachers, principals, and other school leaders should think about when implementing a schoolwide program:

- ✓ Schools should use the SAFE criteria (**S**equentially organized activities, **A**ctive forms of learning, **F**ocus on promoting social competence, and **E**xplicitly target specific social/emotional development skills; Durlak et al., 2011) when evaluating the quality of any schoolwide program they are considering for adoption.

- ✓ Schoolwide programs are as much about organizational or systems change as they are about changing student behavior.

- ✓ Schoolwide change is a collaborative process.

- ✓ Schoolwide social learning programs should be viewed as a long-term process that requires a long-term commitment from all levels of the school system. If both leadership and teachers are not committed to the program, then schools should either build commitment or look at other options.

- ✓ Schools should target 80% buy-in from staff before implementing a program.

- ✓ Expect the start-up phase to last 3–5 years. The 3–5 years will include baseline data collection, training, initial implementation (where people will make mistakes since they are being asked to do something new), trouble-shooting problems that arise, providing feedback and additional practice or training, including additional components (such as parent programs), and finally school staff achieving a level of mastery in their ability to implement the program.

- ✓ Resistance to change is a normal human response. People who exhibit resistance should not be labeled as "problems" or "lazy."

- ✓ Choose a program that provides planning and ongoing support for the 3–5 year roll-out process.

✓ Conduct a needs assessment before choosing a program and then use that assessment data to choose an evidence-based program that best matches the school's needs and goals.

✓ Choose a program that has both good evidence and a solid grounding in theory (i.e., behavioral, social-cognitive, social learning, effective and developmentally appropriate instruction).

✓ When implementing a schoolwide program, schools should monitor both implementation integrity (Is everyone doing what they are supposed to be doing?) and program effectiveness (Is there improvement in student behavior, school climate, and attendance?).

✓ Finally, don't throw the baby out with the bath water. Schoolwide change does not mean scrapping everything a school is doing and starting over. When adopting a schoolwide program, there will be some critical components that are necessary for program success, but there are other parts that schools can customize. School should build on their strengths and keep activities, polices, and programs that are working.

**APPENDIX 3.1. Online Databases That Provide Evaluations
of Research Evidence Available for Schoolwide
(as Well as Classroom- and Individual-Level) Programs**

- The Collaborative for Academic, Social, and Emotional Learning (CASEL) produce the *Safe and Sound Guide* (as well as other reports on social/emotional learning research) evaluating evidence-based programs: *http://casel.org/about-us*.

- Office of Juvenile Justice and Delinquency Prevention has developed a searchable guide of model programs: *www.ojjdp.gov/mpg*.

- The Institute of Behavioral Science at the University of Colorado at Boulder's Center for the Study and Prevention of Violence has reviewed a variety of violence prevention programs (many that focus on building social and emotional development skills) and identified both model and promising programs: *www.colorado.edu/cspv/blueprints*.

- The Substance Abuse and Mental Health Services Association has put together a searchable database, the National Registry of Evidence-based Programs and Practices: *www.nrepp.samhsa.gov*.

- Find Youth Info is a resource created by a working group composed of members from 12 different federal agencies that are responsible for youth support and programming. This website includes an *Evidence and Innovations* tab that contains a searchable program directory of evidence-based programs: *www.findyouthinfo.gov*.

- Institute for Educational Sciences has developed the What Works Clearinghouse to disseminate information about evidence-based programs: *http://ies.ed.gov/ncee/wwc*.

- The Promising Practices Network on children, families, and communities has developed a website to provide information on a variety of different evidence-based practices. Programs are listed so that practitioners can get information on the quality and quantity of evidence-based support by clicking on the program name: *www.promisingpractices.net/programs.asp*.

- One final set of resources for assisting special educators in identifying evidence-based practices can be found on the Council for Exceptional Children's website: *www.cec.sped.org/Standards/Evidence-Based-Practice-Resources-Original?sc_lang=en*. Under *Teaching and Learning Center*, there is a section on evidence-based practices that contains multiple resources describing evidence-based practice and what it means in special education.

CHAPTER 4

Classroom Approaches
to Social Skills Development

Although the importance of social skills is clear, allocating time in the school day to teach them directly through planned instruction can be difficult for classroom teachers. Especially in an educational climate that prioritizes high-stakes academic accountability, social skills instruction in many school districts may fall casualty to an increased focus on standardized testing. Practitioners may find it challenging, and perhaps unrealistic, to spend precious time and limited instructional resources teaching skills that many adults take for granted and consider common sense—and even perceive to be parental responsibility. Yet students, particularly those with disabilities, continue to struggle with their social behaviors in school and nonschool environments. In order to justify spending limited instructional time and resources teaching social competencies in the classroom, it is important to consider and understand how these skills are conceptualized, or interpreted and understood, and the ways in which they influence academic achievement.

The goals of K–12 education are often measured by performance on academic assessments, and given the importance and influence of social behaviors on academic achievement, it is necessary to reflect on the ways in which educators can improve the social skills of young students and thereby their academic accomplishments. Thus, Chapters 1 and 2 reviewed some of the mechanisms, or pathways, through which school performance is influenced by the types of social skills addressed in many of the curricula we present in this chapter.

For students with disabilities, fostering a classroom environment that emphasizes social competence in structured instructional formats is particularly important. Historically, students with disabilities have more difficulty building and maintaining friendships than students without disabilities. Indeed, through research and practice, we know that the quality of one's relationships with peers is a factor in that student's academic and social motivation and later accomplishments (see Parker & Asher, 1987). Thus, students with disabilities may be at further academic disadvantage purely because of their difficulties with social engagements. One way for practitioners to reduce the negative consequences of poor social participation is to formally address, in the classroom, the skills that enable all students to confidently increase their social footprint and meet their peers'—and teachers'—expectations.

By creating an academic and social atmosphere that promotes basic prosocial experiences (e.g., cooperation and relationship building), teachers can provide authentic opportunities for students with disabilities to interact with their peers and for authentic friendships to develop. In an inclusive classroom, positive peer interaction among students with and without disabilities supports a cooperative and accepting environment, which is beneficial to all. Moreover, by addressing the social skills of all students, regardless of ability, teachers will especially improve the school experiences of students with disabilities.

Besides fostering a community environment, teachers who emphasize social competence with their instructional choices help students with disabilities to learn social rules and expectations in safe, nurturing environments and in a context that involves their peers. Many students, not just those with disabilities, struggle to make sense of what they need to do or how they need to act in the various social engagements that take place during a typical school day. Thus, explicitly teaching social skills in the classroom helps all students learn appropriate ways to navigate through these situations while developing skills that will support them in future academic and social endeavors.

In this chapter, we describe a variety of curricula, many of which are used as primary or secondary intervention techniques, that classroom teachers can use to teach social competence in the elementary grades. We have chosen to include those programs that have what we call evidence supporting efficacy. This means that the included curricula, except Social Skills Activities for Special Children, have been demonstrated effective through documented and authentic classroom use or empirical intervention studies or are rooted in theoretical instructional approaches validated by past research. We chose to include Social Skills Activities for Special Children even though it does not meet the evidence requirement because it is a popular and recently updated social skills curriculum supplement that has received numerous positive reviews and has been in continuous publication since its initial release in 1993. Also in this chapter, we present a brief description of evidence-based practice and outline a practitioner guide for determining whether enough evidence exists to designate a curriculum worthy of purchase or implementation.

WHAT DOES "EVIDENCE-BASED PRACTICE" MEAN?

A large, and continually expanding, body of social skills curricula is available from which teachers can choose when preparing their inclusive classrooms for each school year. Yet, with such great breadth in the resources available, how does one select the most suitable from the smorgasbord of published curricula? For the purpose of this chapter, any academic or social program, curriculum, intervention, or prevention plat-form available in a packaged format is referred to as "curricula(um)." When making a choice about which curriculum to adopt and use, teachers sometimes operate under the direction of their school district; in other situations, teachers are able to make these choices on their own. Either way, discussing the merit and evidence base of various published curricula is a worthwhile exercise and will provide the foundation for future discussions of what is best for your individual classroom.

There are two circumstances that typically lead a school district or individual teacher to consider specific curricula: (1) The curriculum has been validated as effective for its intended purposes through research and/or (2) the curriculum is in widespread use. Different criteria can be used to determine whether a curriculum is considered effective. Multiple positive teacher testimonials are one source of validation of a curric-ulum's effectiveness. More formally, however, validation comes in the form of research findings that demonstrate significant improvements in student performance that are directly tied to the curriculum in question. Data-based research findings, published in peer-reviewed journals, are considered "evidence" of effectiveness. Evidence of effec-tiveness is an especially relevant notion in today's educational climate. Federal and state legislation place a premium on the use of curricula with an evidence base determined by findings from rigorous scientific inquiry.

Evidence-based practices are supported by rigorous and systematic scientific inquiry, meaning that the curriculum in question has been tested with an authentic audience (target population) usually through multiple randomized controlled trials. A randomized controlled trial is a study in which the researchers place students (either individually or by classroom or by school) randomly into either an intervention group (the group that receives the curricula being tested) or a control group (the group that does not receive the curricula in question). The effects of the curricula can, therefore, be measured by assessing the difference in outcomes between the two groups.

For example, if a new social skills curriculum emphasizing cooperation is devel-oped, researchers may decide to test the efficacy of the curriculum. To test its efficacy, or how well it improves cooperation skills, the new curriculum is implemented with groups of students. First, the students' skill level on the outcome variable of interest would be assessed (in this example, cooperation skills). Ideally, students would then be randomly assigned to either an intervention or a control group. We might imagine that the intervention is used with one of the groups of students—the intervention group—for 60 days. Another equal-sized group of students—the control group—would not be exposed to the new cooperation curriculum. At the end of the 60-day period, all of the students, in both the intervention and the control groups, receive some form of assess-ment that measures individual levels of cooperation. If gains in cooperation skills are found among the students in the intervention group but not the control group, and these gains are statistically significant, then there is evidence that this cooperation cur-riculum is effective for improving student cooperation skills.

Of course, this is a rather simplified example; many variables would need to be con-sidered and controlled during the course of research. However, it highlights the prem-ise of randomized control trials, the gold-standard method of conducting an empirical research study aimed at determining the efficacy of an intervention.

Identifying Evidence-Based Practices

Teachers do not always have carte blanche to choose curriculum, but they can identify and evaluate whether the curriculum material to which they have been given access are evidence based and supported by scientific research. Evaluating a curriculum can be simplified by following three steps outlined in the Coalition for Evidence-Based Policy (2003) publication *Identifying and Implementing Educational Practices Supported by Rigorous Evidence.*

The first step is to determine whether the curriculum in question is supported by substantial evidence of efficacy. To evaluate this, teachers must consider both the quality of research that investigates the curriculum as well as the quantity of proof. For example, a high-quality research study typically utilizes randomized controlled trials that are implemented with fidelity, that is, trustworthiness and reliability. In terms of quantity, the curriculum should be found effective in more than one setting similar to the one in which a contemplating teacher plans to implement it. High quality and frequency of use are paramount to determining satisfactory or substantial evidence of efficacy.

The second step in the process of evaluating curricula involves the search for *potential* evidence of efficacy. If a search does not uncover strong (substantial) evidence during step 1, other forms of research evidence could also be considered acceptable as potential evidence of effectiveness. Randomized controlled trials are not always feasible in authentic education settings. Therefore, another popular research design used by researchers to understand the effectiveness of a particular intervention or curriculum is known as comparison group studies. Implementation of comparison group studies involves comparing the effectiveness of a particular curriculum between two groups not selected by randomization. For example, it is often difficult and unrealistic to randomly select students in a school to participate in an experimental intervention since students are "bounded" by their classrooms. Therefore, rather than random placement of individual students, it is more feasible to choose which classrooms receive the intervention. Also known as quasi-experimental design, this method of investigation is not considered as rigorous as randomized controlled trials, because participants are not randomly assigned to groups, and thus an increase in performance could potentially be the result of context variables rather than the intervention.

Randomization is a core quality of being able to generalize the effects of the curriculum in question. If, on the other hand, participants are not assigned randomly to the intervention and control groups, it is possible to question whether gains were made due to the curriculum or to differences between the groups of students in each condition. According to the Coalition for Evidence-Based Policy (2003), quasi-experimental designs can still produce valid evidence for determining the effectiveness of curriculum; however, it is still recommended that results of these studies be confirmed through replications or randomized controlled trails.

The third and final step in evaluating curricula is to establish a conclusion about whether the curriculum is, in fact, supported by evidence. If the answer is "no" to both steps 1 and 2, then it can be concluded that the curriculum is not evidence based. However, it is important to note that not all effective curricula have an empirical evidence base. Some social skills interventions, in fact, have been tested and used for years—with measurable results—without formal research support. If you are interested in curricula that match this description, our advice is to seek as much evidence as possible that can attest to the efficacy of the intervention in question, including teacher support. Contacting the publisher of the curricula may result in acquiring more proof of effectiveness than is readily found online or in professional publications.

Why Is the Evidence-Based Practice Label Important?

Research supported evidence is important for a number of reasons: (1) Students deserve access to curricula that are effective; (2) teachers cannot afford to spend time with a curriculum that simply doesn't work; and (3) with limited and often decreasing fiscal resources, taking financial risk on classroom materials that have not been validated as worthwhile makes little sense. Furthermore, federal and state policies dictate a preference for teachers to use instructional materials and curricula that are supported by rigorous, scientific research.

Although the moniker "evidence-based practice" is an important one, all of the curricula presented in this chapter are unable to meet the technical criteria for this label. Some included programs have not been field tested in a controlled research environment or been demonstrated effective by published research results. Thus, they are not supported by the evidence-based requirement of peer-reviewed research. To be considered empirically evidence based, research supporting the curricula needs to be peer reviewed and published, most often in an academic research journal. Curricula without this research support, however, can still be considered valuable. Rather than rely on controlled environment testing, some curricula are developed with theoretical and empirical backing and thus demonstrate effectiveness by containing systematic strategies and intervention techniques that have substantial empirical support (e.g., cooperative learning, cognitive-behavioral therapy, and aggression replacement therapy). To be all inclusive of curricula that we believe useful and worthwhile, we have included those programs with both immediate empirical support with peer-reviewed results and those which contain empirically based strategies and techniques.

METHODOLOGY FOR INCLUDING CURRICULA

We selected curricula to be included in this chapter that (1) focus on the social skills development of elementary school students and (2) were designed predominantly for implementation at the classroom level (as primary or secondary interventions). The included curricula are currently in publication or are readily available for purchase individually or in complete classroom sets. With the exception of one curriculum, Social Skills Activities for Special Children, we highlight only those published social skills interventions with some form of available documented evidence base. To garner evidence, we relied on extensive academic database searches and contact with the program's publisher. Following each program description is a section titled "Sample of Evidence Supporting Efficacy." For these interventions, there exists empirical research that supports implementation of the curricula or empirical research and field experience that supports the theoretical frameworks behind the curricula (e.g., instructional methods and techniques). References and citations relating to the empirical evidence of each program are also provided. Citations marked *indirect* reflect support of theoretical components of the curricula. See Table 4.1 for a visual resource of the included programs.

Al's Pals: Kids Making Healthy Choices

Author: Susan R. Geller, MS

Publication Date: 1993

Publisher: Wingspan, LLC

Website: *www.wingspanworks.com*

Al's Pals is an early childhood intervention and prevention curriculum designed for promoting prosocial development in young children. It is a resiliency-framed curriculum that emphasizes personal, social, and emotional skill development through interactive and activity-based lessons. Specifically, this program assists children between the ages of 3 and 8 in acquiring the skills necessary for (1) appropriate emotional regulation, (2) interacting with others, (3) accepting academic and social differences, (4) self-control, (5) conflict resolution, and (6) making good choices.

Al's Pals includes a substantial teacher training component, an element that details teacher strategies for turning classrooms into safe and healthy environments that foster compassion, cooperation, respect, and responsibility. It should be noted that Al's Pals was created in response to a mounting concern about preschool children who displayed antisocial behaviors, including aggression and noncompliance.

By applying a resiliency research framework, the author developed this program to address poor behavior while simultaneously teaching prosocial life skills. The curriculum has since been modified for use in elementary classrooms and has been validated through age 8. A supplemental strength-based parent guide for improving relationships between students and their parents is also available. The training for Al's Pals is delivered by its national distributor, Wingspan, and is required for all practitioners planning to implement the curriculum. The Al's Pals curriculum aligns with the resiliency-focused conceptualization of social competence we discussed in Chapter 2.

Sample of Evidence Supporting Efficacy

Lynch, K. B., Geller, S. R., & Schmidt, M. G. (2004). Multi-year evaluation of the effectiveness of a resilience-based prevention program for young children. *Journal of Primary Prevention, 24*, 335–353.

Connecting with Others: Lessons for Teaching Social and Emotional Competence: K–2, 3–5

Author: Rita Coombs-Richardson, PhD

Publication Date: 1996

Publisher: Research Press

Website: *www.researchpress.com*

TABLE 4.1. Effective Social Skills Curricula Guide for Elementary Classrooms

Title	Author	Publisher	Date	Targeted skills	Website
Al's Pals: Kids Making Healthy Choices	Gellar	Wingspan	1993	Appropriate emotional regulation, interacting with others, accepting differences, self-control, conflict resolution, making good choices	www.wingspanworks.com
Connecting with Others: Lessons for Teaching Social and Emotional Competence	Coombs-Richardson	Research Press	1996	Effective communication, self-advocacy, interpersonal and problem-solving skills	www.researchpress.com
"I Can Problem Solve!" An Interpersonal Cognitive Problem-Solving Program	Shure	Research Press	2001	Aims to change how students think instead of how to behave; vocabulary component for strengthening effective and appropriate communication	www.researchpress.com
The Incredible Years: Dina Dinosaur Child Training Program	Webster-Stratton	Incredible Years, Inc.	1992	Making and maintaining friends, communication, problem solving, anger management, conflict remediation, listening and following rules	www.incredibleyears.com
Making Choices: Social Problem-Solving Skills for Children	Fraser, Nash, Galinsky, & Darwin	National Association of Social Workers Press	2000	Cooperation, assessment of various situations and environments, relevant goal setting, group participation skills	www.naswpress.org
Open Circle Curriculum	Seigle, Lange, & Macklem	Open Circle, Wellesley Centers for Women, Wellesley College	1987	Effective communication, group problem solving, self-awareness, self-management, social awareness, relationship development and maintenance, responsible decision making	www.open-circle.org
Prepare Curriculum: Teaching Prosocial Competencies	Goldstein	Research Press	1999	Aggression, stress, prejudice reduction, group investigation, decision making, and action related to classroom and community problems or issues	www.researchpress.com

Title	Author	Publisher	Year	Skills	Website
Promoting Social Success: A Curriculum for Children with Special Needs	Siperstein & Rickards	Brookes	2003	Independent thinking, problem solving, understanding and regulating emotions, making and keeping friends, recognizing conflict	www.brookespublishing.com
Second Step: Skills for Social and Academic Success	Committee for Children	Committee for Children	1989	Paying attention, listening, being assertive, ignoring distractions, staying on task, getting along with others, emotional regulation, cooperation, problem solving	www.cfchildren.org
Skillstreaming the Elementary School Child: A Guide for Teaching Prosocial Skills	McGinnis	Research Press	2011	Self-control, conflict management, recognizing personal and others' emotions, responding to teasing, dealing with group pressure, making friends	www.researchpress.com
Skillstreaming in the Elementary School: Lesson Plans and Activities	McGinnis	Research Press	2005	Self-advocacy, asking questions, setting goals, communication, admitting mistakes, self-control, dealing with stress	www.researchpress.com
Social Skills Activities for Special Children	Mannix	Jossey-Bass	1993 2008	Accepting rules and authority at school, making and keeping friends, getting along with peers, understanding social cues and situations, working in groups	www.josseybass.com
Social Skills in Pictures, Stories, and Songs: A Multisensory Program for Preschool and Early Elementary Students	Serna, Nielsen, & Forness	Research Press	2007	Following direction, sharing, managing personal behavior, problem solving	www.researchpress.com
Stop & Think Social Skills Program	Knoff	Sopris West Educational Services	2001	Interpersonal, problem solving, conflict resolution, listening, ignoring distractions, accepting consequences, setting goals, handling peer pressure	www.projectachieve.info
Tough Kid Social Skills Book	Sheridan	Pacific Northwest	2010	Recognizing and expressing emotions appropriately, conversation, self-control, cooperation, problem solving, participating in groups, accepting "no"	www.pacificnwpublish.com

Connecting with Others is a school-based social and emotional curriculum that helps students develop communication, self-advocacy, interpersonal, and problem-solving skills. Through systematic and planned instruction, students learn to accept differences, resolve conflicts, and communicate effectively in both social and academic climates. The foundational belief behind this curriculum is that these skills are paramount to children's socioemotional health and, in turn, school success. The original purpose of this program was to prepare students with disabilities for social situations in inclusive classrooms.

Connecting with Others is applicable to students across age, grade, and ability. The curriculum has been successfully modified to accommodate students both with and without disabilities and incudes 30 lessons that each focus on a specific skill set, organized into six themes: (1) concept of self and others, (2) socialization, (3) problem solving and conflict resolution, (4) communication, (5) sharing, and (6) empathy and caring. The lessons include direct instruction scripts for teachers and activities, which can be modified contingent on group or individual needs. Multiple instructional approaches, which emphasize active participation and generalization to real-world contexts, are used in this curriculum. A few of the frequently relied-upon strategies include cooperative learning, storytelling, behavioral rehearsal, modeling, creative expression, journaling, and community involvement.

It is advised that teachers present these social skills lessons three times each week to ensure consistent student learning and performance. Also, it is valuable to note that this curriculum can be used as a stand-alone program or infused into other content areas, such as language arts, history, or health education. The Connecting with Others curriculum addresses the various components that fall under the socioemotional competence framework we presented in Chapter 2.

Sample of Evidence Supporting Efficacy

Richardson, R. C., Myran, S. P., & Tonelsone, S. (2009). Teaching social and emotional competence in early childhood. *Journal of International Special Education, 24*, 143–149.

Schultz, B. L., Richardson, R. C., Barber, C. R., & Wilcox, D. (2011). A preschool pilot study of "Connecting with Others: Lessons for Teaching Social and Emotional Competence." *Early Childhood Education Journal, 39*, 143–148.

"I Can Problem Solve!" An Interpersonal Cognitive Problem-Solving Program

Author: Myrna B. Shure, PhD

Publication Date: 2001

Publisher: Research Press

Website: *www.researchpress.com*

"I Can Problem Solve!" is a school-based intervention and prevention program that helps children develop the necessary skills for solving problems in a variety of social settings. Specifically, students learn how to (1) critically generate solutions to various types of problems, (2) think about and cognitively outline consequences before making decisions, and (3) recognize personal as well as peers' emotions. The underlying focus of "I Can Problem Solve" is to teach students to think about and plan out their actions in stages rather than simply teach behavior. Through this framework, by changing students' compulsive thinking processes, impulsivity is reduced and social adjustment and prosocial behaviors improve. Multiple instructional methods are utilized in this program, including games, stories, puppets, and role plays, all of which are implemented in ways relevant to young students' lives (e.g., playground experiences and classroom situations).

The "I Can Problem Solve!" curriculum begins with vocabulary lessons for strengthening effective and appropriate communication skills, which are highly valued when solving problems in group contexts. For example, problem-solving language such as "if–then" are gateway concepts for understanding the consequences of actions. Altogether, there are 77 lessons organized into five units: (1) Pre-Problem-Solving Skills, (2) Alternative Solutions, (3) Consequences, (4) Solution–Consequence Pairs, and (5) Means–Ends Thinking. This activity-heavy curriculum is designed to be engaging and fun, for use as a specific social skills curriculum or supplemental in the context of other subject areas. "I Can Problem Solve!" is aimed at the more general school participation conceptualizations of social competence, such as the skills through which students are able to strengthen their relationships with others and thus increase their attachment to school.

Sample of Evidence Supporting Efficacy

Boyle, D., & Hassett-Walker, C. (2008). Reducing overt and relational aggression among young children: The results from a two-year outcome evaluation. *Journal of School Violence 7*(1), 27–42.

The Incredible Years: Dina Dinosaur Child Training Program

Author: Carolyn Webster-Stratton, PhD, FAAN

Publication Date: 1992

Publisher: The Incredible Years, Inc.

Website: *www.incredibleyears.com*

The Incredible Years is designed as an intervention and prevention curriculum for promoting healthy social competence development and thereby reducing or eliminating conduct problems among children between the ages of 2 and 10. The curriculum utilizes multiple instructional strategies such as video modeling, group discussion, and rehearsal intervention for providing intensive services to youth with moderate to severe problem behavior. As a twofold program, reduction of problem behaviors is directly related to the increase in children's social abilities, their awareness of emotion, conflict management, and school engagement. In this intervention framework, *school engagement* is a term that encompasses academic readiness and cooperation with both peers and adults.

The Incredible Years school-based program is intended to be implemented as either a stand-alone curriculum for classroom use or a pull-out program for individual students or small groups. Students participate in learning activities that fall under three themes: (1) social skills, including communication and friendship; (2) problem solving, including anger management and interpersonal conflict remediation skills; and (3) classroom behavior, including listening and compliance.

Each curriculum package contains 13 videotapes, a comprehensive leader manual with discussion questions and reproducible handouts, cue cards, homework activities, and children's books. This specific Incredible Years program is one in a series of three. The other two programs involve parent and teacher-specific components and activities that augment the curriculum. It should be noted that the series was awarded the 1997 U.S. Leila Rowland National Mental Health Award for exceptional prevention curriculum. As a stand-alone program, the Incredible Years school-based curriculum addresses multiple conceptualizations of social competence, including the skills that promote school readiness, emotional competency, and psychological well-being.

Sample of Evidence Supporting Efficacy

Hutchings, J., Bywater, T., Daley, D., & Lane, E. (2007). A pilot study of the Webster-Stratton Incredible Years Therapeutic Dinosaur School programme. *Clinical Psychology Forum, 170*, 21–24.

Larsson, B., Fossum, S., Clifford, G., Drugli, M. B., Handegard, B. H., & Morch, W. (2008). Treatment of oppositional defiant and conduct problems in young Norwegian children. *European Child and Adolescent Psychiatry, 18*(1), 42–52.

Webster-Stratton, C., Reid, J. M., & Stoolmiller, M. (2008). Preventing conduct problems and improving school readiness: Evaluation of the Incredible Years Teacher and child training programs in high-risk schools. *Journal of Child Psychology and Psychiatry, 49*, 471–488.

Making Choices: Social Problem-Solving Skills for Children

Authors: Mark W. Fraser, PhD, James K. Nash, PhD, Maeda J. Galinsky, PhD, and Kathleen M. Darwin, MSW

Publication Date: 2000

Publisher: National Association of Social Workers Press

Website: *www.naswpress.org*

Making Choices: Social Problem-Solving Skills for Children is designed for use with all students, regardless of disability status, as both a whole-class application and within small groups. The curriculum includes specific strategies that address behaviors of students who are chronically disruptive or have severe behavior problems. Making Choices utilizes a cognitive problem-solving approach and relies heavily on research that underscores the importance of encoding and interpreting social cues. A defining characteristic of this program is the flexibility it affords teachers. For example, this curriculum encourages the implementer to present the lesson plans and activities in ways that are relevant to the immediate context in which it is applied and that foster culturally responsible teaching and learning.

The authors of Making Choices assert that the skills emphasized in this program lay the foundation for developing and maintaining students' relationships with peers and adults across a lifetime. A focus of this curriculum, cooperation, enables children to develop the necessary skills for working well with others in academic, social, and future employment domains. Specifically, and in a nutshell, this program teaches students to assess a variety of situations and environments, set relevant and appropriate social goals, and participate amicably in group social and learning activities.

Making Choices consists of 29 individual lessons that fit into seven units organized by theme: (1) Learning about Emotions and Feelings; (2) Encoding: Identifying Social Cues; (3) Interpretation: Making Sense of Social Cues; (4) Goal Formulation and Refinement: Setting Social Goals; (5) Response Search and Formulation: Inventing Options; (6) Response Decision: Making a Choice; and (7) Enacting: Acting on Choices. It should be noted that when used exclusively with students who have severe conduct problems, the authors suggest that Making Choices be combined with another curriculum that specifically targets the behavioral risk factors associated with conduct disorder.

Making Choices is another curriculum example of a formal instructional program that targets multiple conceptualizations of social competence, including social skills, academic enablers, and behavior control. There is a strong focus on emotional and personal aspects of social competence; thus, this curriculum can be regarded as primarily attending to the emotional and psychological constructs of social competencies.

Sample of Evidence Supporting Efficacy

Fraser, M. W., Galinsky, M. J., Smokowski, P. R., Day, S. H., Terzian, M. A., Rose, R. A., et al. (2005). Social information-processing skills training to promote social competence and prevent aggressive behaviors in the third grades. *Journal of Consulting and Clinical Psychology, 73*(6), 1045–1055.

Open Circle Curriculum

Authors: Pamela Seigle, MS, Lois Lange, MSW, and Gayle Macklem, MA, LEP

Publication Date: 1987

Publisher: Open Circle, Wellesley Centers for Women, Wellesley College

Website: *www.open-circle.org*

Open Circle is designed to promote social and emotional learning in kindergarten through grade 5. Rooted in principles related to cooperative learning (further elaborated in Chapter 5), Open Circle stresses the importance of cooperation and teamwork. The goal of this program is to encourage young students to develop social competencies such as effective communication skills and group problem-solving skills. By using this curriculum, teachers help students learn how to express themselves appropriately through language and action. Additionally, students learn to work collaboratively with others as part of a cohesive team. Specific competencies targeted by Open Circle include (1) self-awareness, (2) self-management, (3) social awareness, (4) relationship development and maintenance, and (5) responsible decision making.

Open Circle contains 42 primary lessons organized into three parts: (1) creating a cooperative classroom environment, (2) building self-esteem and positive relationships, and (3) solving people problems. In addition, the curriculum provides 33 supplemental lessons that range in focus from peer pressure to alternative thinking. It should be noted that the Open Circle curriculum is considered both a classroom curriculum and a schoolwide program. Although it is presented as an option for implementation at the whole-school level in promotional material, its core learning components are delivered through classroom-based lesson plans. Open Circle approaches social competence from a psychological framework, in that many of the skills targeted fall under what we identified in Chapter 2 as a psychological umbrella.

Sample of Evidence Supporting Efficacy

Hennessey, B. A. (2007). Promoting social competence in school aged children: The effects of the open circle program. *Journal of School Psychology, 45*, 349–360.

Taylor, C. A., Liang, B., Tracy, A. J., Williams, L. M., & Seigle, P. (2002). Gender differences in middle school adjustment, physical fighting, and social skills: Evaluation of a social competency program. *Journal of Primary Prevention, 23*(2), 259–272.

Prepare Curriculum: Teaching Prosocial Competencies

Author: Arnold P. Goldstein, PhD

Publication Date: 1999

Publisher: Research Press

Website: *www.researchpress.com*

The Prepare Curriculum was originally developed for use at the middle and secondary level but has been revised and modified to accommodate students in the elementary classroom. The Prepare Curriculum is school based and focuses on enhancing prosocial behaviors through three units: (1) Reducing Aggression, (2) Reducing Stress, and (3) Reducing Prejudice among Youth. Each unit utilizes cooperative learning as a primary vehicle for teaching desirable behaviors. Some focal concepts include group investigation of a problem, group decision making, group action, and group reflection.

Cooperative team gaming and classroom tournaments are used as part of the curriculum to cultivate an atmosphere of collaboration where self-improvement is emphasized with peer (teammate) supports. The curriculum is composed of 93 interactive lessons and includes exercises that promote student participation and leadership. Besides cooperative gaming, the program lessons and activities include role-play, reading and writing, drawing, group discussion, photography, tape-recording, and multiple other interactive hands-on activities.

Through fun and engaging learning activities, students develop prosocial psychological and emotional competencies needed for academic and social success. To that end, students learn how to manage their behaviors, assess a variety of social situations, and maintain their newly developed skills. The Prepare Curriculum addresses psychological interpretations of social competence by way of strengthening students' personal identification with various prosocial behaviors.

Sample of Evidence Supporting Efficacy: Indirect

Amendola, A. M., & Oliver, R. W. (2003). LSCI and aggression replacement training: A multi-modal approach. *Reclaiming Children and Youth, 12*(3), 181–185.

Barnoski, R., & Aos, S. (2004). *Outcome evaluation of Washington State's research-based programs for juvenile offenders* (section 4, pp. 9–12). Olympia: Washington State Institute for Public Policy.

Lochman, J. E. (1992). Cognitive-behavioral intervention with aggressive boys: Three-year follow-up and preventive effects. *Journal of Consulting and Clinical Psychology, 60*(3), 426–432.

Wilson, D. B., Bouffard, L. A., & Mackenzie, D. L. (2005). A quantitative review of structured, group-oriented, cognitive-behavioral programs for offenders. *Criminal Justice and Behavior, 32*(2), 172–204.

Promoting Social Success: A Curriculum for Children with Special Needs

Authors: Gary N. Siperstein, PhD, and Emily Paige Rickards, MA

Publication Date: 2003

Publisher: Brookes

Promoting Social Success helps students with disabilities develop many of the social skills required to succeed in a variety of social situations in inclusive elementary classrooms. Instead of focusing on the teaching of behavior, this curriculum emphasizes cognitive procedures that theoretically influence behavior. Specifically, the units in this program teach children how to think independently and problem solve so that they are adequately prepared for a variety of social situations. Promoting Social Success is designed to improve social skills by way of enhancing students' cognitive processing skills.

The curriculum guide contains a total of 66 lesson plans with multiple reproducible activities. Each lesson plan is expected to take between 30 and 45 minutes to implement, a duration that makes teaching social skills feasible in a busy academic school day. Split into five units, the lesson plans are grouped according to theme: (1) Introduction (to the program as well as to peers via ice breaker activities); (2) Understanding Feelings and

Actions: Emotional and Behavioral Regulation; (3) Using Social Information: Noticing and Interpreting Cues; (4) Planning What to Do: Problem Solving; and (5) Making and Keeping Friends: Social Knowledge.

Each lesson plan includes a description of (1) the day's focus, (2) what the students will accomplish, (3) the materials needed, (4) the accompanying activity, and (5) how to wrap up the lesson. Each lesson plan also contains options and suggestions for alternative presentation. Promoting Social Success targets multiple conceptualizations of social competence, including basic social skills, emotional awareness and regulation, and psychological well-being. Students with these qualities often feel more attachment to school than do their peers who lack or struggle in these domains.

Sample of Evidence Supporting Efficacy: Indirect

Dodge, K. A., & Price, J. M. (1994). On the relation between social information processing and socially competent behavior in early school-aged children. *Child Development, 65,* 1385–1397.

Second Step: Skills for Social and Academic Success

Author: Committee for Children

Publication Date: 1989

Publisher: Committee for Children

Website: *www.cfchildren.org/second-step.aspx*

Second Step: Skills for Social and Academic Success is another curriculum that can be used as a primary intervention in either classroom or schoolwide application. In this chapter, we present Second Step from a classroom use perspective. Second Step addresses skills for reducing aggressive or impulsive behaviors by teaching specific social and emotional competencies. It can be considered a prevention program, rather than an intervention, because many of the skills addressed would be considered to prevent long-term behavior problems. Thus, implementation of Second Step allows students to learn and practice the social tools they need to become successful in school settings before undesirable behaviors are able to manifest. By emphasizing "skills for learning" (i.e., paying attention, listening, being assertive and ignoring distractions), this curriculum teaches students how to navigate the many social situations and expectations they encounter during a typical school day.

Two of the primary themes emphasized through this program are staying on task and getting along with others. To that end, Second Step helps students learn how to respond empathetically to their peers, regulate their emotions, manage their feelings, and problem solve. Additionally, students participate in a "thinking critically" component that promotes team building and cooperative decision making.

The individual lessons in this curriculum are expected to take about 25–30 minutes each and can be implemented either as stand-alone or in conjunction with a content area. Practitioners are advised to plan at least 20 weeks to complete the entire program. Second Step addresses the socioemotional framework of social competence, in that the skills it emphasizes are strongly correlated with controlling, recognizing, and responding appropriately to various states of emotion.

Sample of Evidence Supporting Efficacy

Grossman, D. C., Neckerman, H. J., Koepsell, T. D., Liu, P. Y., Asher, K. N., Beland, K., et al. (1997). Effectiveness of a violence prevention curriculum among children in elementary school: A randomized control trial. *Journal of the American Medical Association, 277*, 1605–1611.

Holsen, I., Smith, B., & Frey, K. S. (2008). Outcomes of the social competence program "Second Step" in Norwegian elementary schools. *School Psychology International, 29*(1), 71–88.

Holsen, I., Iversen, A. C., & Smith, B. (2009). Universal social competence programme in school: Does it work for children with low socio-economic background? *Advances in School Mental Health Promotion, 2*(2), 51–60.

Skillstreaming the Elementary School Child: A Guide for Teaching Prosocial Skills (3rd Edition)

Author: Ellen McGinnis, PhD

Publication Date: 2011

Publisher: Research Press

Website: *www.researchpress.com*

Skillstreaming the Elementary School Child is designed to address problem behaviors exhibited by students in grades 2 to 5. Students who display aggressive and immature behaviors as well as those who are withdrawn in social situations benefit most from this program. Skillstreaming employs a skill-deficit model, which identifies the social skills students are lacking and then targets those skills for improvement through specific intervention techniques by way of planned and systematically implemented direct instruction. Skillstreaming is strongly focused on serving individual student need.

Four specific evidence-based techniques are utilized in the Skillstreaming program: (1) modeling, (2) role-playing, (3) consistent and constant feedback, and (4) programming for generalization. The curriculum is both an intervention and preventive effort; by teaching students certain necessary skills for maneuvering through social situations, the instructional methods target already occurring behavior while also preventing further poor behaviors from manifesting.

Through participation in this program, students develop self-control skills designed to help them become capable of appropriately managing interpersonal conflicts. Some of the targeted skills include recognizing feelings, responding to teasing, and dealing with group pressure. Skillstreaming consists of 60 lessons organized into five themes:

(1) Classroom Survival Skills, (2) Friendship-Making Skills, (3) Skills for Dealing with Feelings, (4) Skill Alternatives to Aggression, and (5) Skills for Dealing with Stress. Skillstreaming addresses both the general social and socioemotional conceptualizations of social competence, as developing "social knowledge" is strongly emphasized.

Sample of Evidence Supporting Efficacy

Rahill, S. A., & Teglasi, H. (2003). Processes and outcomes of story-based and skill-based social competency programs for children with emotional disabilities. *Journal of School Psychology, 41*, 413–429.

Sheridan, B. A., MacDonald, D. A., Donlon, M., Kuhn, B., McGovern, K., & Friedman, H. (2011). Evaluation of a social skills program based on social learning theory, implemented in a school setting. *Psychological Reports, 108*, 420–436.

Skillstreaming in the Elementary School: Lesson Plans and Activities

Author: Ellen McGinnis, PhD

Publication Date: 2005

Publisher: Research Press

Website: *www.skillstreaming.com*

The Skillstreaming lesson plan and activity guide is a continuation of the skills and strategy curriculum Skillstreaming the Elementary School Child (McGinnis, 2011), described previously. It was developed to supplement the first by offering additional strategies and learning activities for either whole-class or smaller, skill-focused group applications. These additional applications would be considered secondary interventions, that is, interventions designed to address the social skills needs of students who were not served adequately by the primary level intervention implemented at the whole-class level.

Intended to provide teachers with additional methods of introducing certain skill sets and to build from skills already in place, this curriculum helps maintain and enhance student competence in social contexts. The activities in this book were developed to be used in conjunction with the five units offered in Skillstreaming the Elementary School Child. To that end, this guide offers practitioners familiar with the Skillstreaming program options for tailoring a curriculum that fits best in their classrooms. Additionally, this guide is accompanied by supplemental electronic materials, including reproducible forms, charts, and worksheets relevant to the Skillstreaming curriculum.

Sample of Evidence Supporting Efficacy

Lerner, M. D., & Mikami, A. Y. (2012). A preliminary randomized controlled trial of two social skills interventions for youth with high-functioning autism spectrum disorders. *Focus on Autism and Other Developmental Disabilities, 27*(3), 147–157.

Sheridan, B. A., MacDonald, D. A., Donlon, M., Kuhn, B., McGovern, K., & Friedman, H. (2011). Evaluation of a social skills program based on social learning theory, implemented in a school setting. *Psychological Reports, 108*, 420–436.

Social Skills Activities for Special Children (2nd Edition)

Author: Darlene Mannix, MA

Publication Date: 2008

Publisher: Jossey-Bass

Website: *josseybasseducation.com*

Social Skills Activities for Special Children is a teaching guide that contains an assortment of lessons, activities, and ideas for assisting elementary grade students with disabilities develop appropriate social and emotional skills. A unique characteristic of this guide is that it focuses on helping students with disabilities become aware of behavior before setting out to change their behavior. In this framework, the awareness component is a key ingredient in helping students develop acceptable behavioral habits that last.

It is important to note that this curriculum supplement has dual objectives. First, it guides teachers in helping students with disabilities think about what social skills are and why they are necessary for school success. Second, it is also an activity resource book, filled with engaging activities for students to use when discussing, thinking about, and practicing social skills. Ultimately, Social Skills Activities for Special Children facilitates student awareness and authentic and relevant opportunities for social skills practice that prepares students with disabilities to succeed in social and emotional situations.

The program consists of 142 individual lessons organized into three sections. Section 1—Accepting Rules and Authority at School—covers four themes: (1) understanding the teacher's role, (2) classroom rules and responsibilities, (3) other authority figures, and (4) when you have problems. Section 2, Relating to Peers, is organized based on three themes: (1) learning and working with others, (2) making friends, and (3) keeping friends. Section 3, Developing Positive Social Skills, consists of four themes: (1) understanding social situations correctly, (2) positive personality attributes, (3) getting along with others, and (4) everyday etiquette.

Also, Social Skills Activities for Special Children contains suggestions for communicating with parents in order to promote students' awareness of appropriate behavior at home as well. Included in the guide are reproducible letters to parents, which are designed to allow teachers to easily keep parents and guardians informed about the social skills awareness and development that is being emphasized in the classroom. Besides providing parents with information about their child's learning during school, these letters contain maintenance and continuity strategies for parents to implement after school. In sum, Social Skills Activities for Special Children strengthens the general social skill and socioemotional domains of social competence by way of engaging, simple lesson activities.

Sample of Evidence Supporting Efficacy

Because *Social Skills Activities for Special Children* is a book of guides, suggestions, and ideas rather than an entire packaged curriculum, it has not been empirically tested as one unit and therefore we are unable to provide a research citation. We included it because of its applicability to classrooms wherein daily activities for improving social skills are warranted, but perhaps a structured curriculum is not feasible and overwhelmingly positive teacher testimonials.

Social Skills in Pictures, Stories, and Songs: A Multisensory Program for Preschool and Early Elementary Students

Authors: Loretta A. Serna, PhD, M. Elizabeth Nielsen, PhD, and Steven R. Forness, PhD

Publication Date: 2007

Publisher: Research Press

Website: *www.researchpress.com*

Social Skills in Pictures, Stories, and Songs is both a social and an emotional skills curriculum geared specifically toward students in the early elementary school grades. It is designed to provide developmental support in the domains of social and emotional health so that students are able to successfully navigate the social and emotional experiences in the early grades. Teachers implement the curriculum through a combination of multiple sensory modalities, including stories, mnemonics, coloring books, songs, role-playing, and a variety of visual stimulants.

Specifically, Social Skills in Pictures, Stories, and Songs is based on four original stories and songs and features original characters delivering prosocial themes: (1) Rosie the Roadrunner, who learns to follow directions; (2) Prairie Dog Pete, who learns to share; (3) Roscoe the Raccoon, who learns to manage his behavior; and (4) Prickles the Porcupine, who learns to solve problems. The curriculum package includes a storybook, original music CD, and an implementation guide for teachers and 10 coloring books, which accompany each of the four stories, for students. The implementation guide offers step-by-step directions for each lesson, but also allows for program modification by the teacher if desired.

Teachers or other instructional staff can adapt the program in order to best fit the context in which their students are learning prosocial behaviors. Of note is that the curriculum is designed to be used in both school and other child care learning settings and has been clinically supported in Head Start classrooms. Social Skills in Pictures, Stories, and Songs addresses the social and socioemotional interpretations of social competence we presented in Chapter 2 by focusing on skills designed to foster students' positive classroom social experiences with their peers and teachers.

Sample of Evidence Supporting Efficacy

Serna, L. A., Nielsen, M. E., Lambros, K., & Forness, S. R. (2000). Primary prevention with children at risk for emotional or behavioral disorders: Data on a universal intervention for Head Start classrooms. *Behavioral Disorders, 26,* 70–84.

Serna, L. A., Forness, S. R., & Gullett, S. (2004, April). *A story-telling intervention for young children: Five years of research.* Paper presented at the annual International Conference of the Council for Exceptional Children, New Orleans, LA.

Stop & Think Social Skills Program

Author: Howard M. Knoff, PhD

Publication Date: 2001

Publisher: Sopris West Educational Services

Website: *www.projectachieve.info/stop-think/stop-and-think.html*

The Stop & Think Social Skills Program has a strong evidence-based history, having been supported by the U.S. Department of Health and Human Services, U.S. Department of Justice, and Collaborative for Social, Emotional, and Academic Learning. Designed for use in pre-K through grade 8, teachers can utilize this curriculum to teach children interpersonal, problem-solving, and conflict resolution strategies. Because of the wide range of ages accommodated by Stop & Think, material for each grade level is packaged separately and designed to be age sensitive and developmentally appropriate for the targeted grades. Ten "core" and 10 "advanced" skills are emphasized at each grade level. These skills assist students in managing personal behaviors and engaging appropriately with peers and adults. Specific skills emphasized in this curriculum include (1) listening, (2) following directions, (3) asking for help, (4) ignoring distractions, (5) accepting consequences, (6) apologizing, (7) dealing with teasing, (8) handling peer pressure, and (9) settings goals. Stop & Think is school based and designed to be implemented in inclusive general education classrooms by both general and special education teachers.

For students with significant social skill needs, this program has the flexibility to be altered so that the material can be delivered as a secondary, or even tertiary, intervention, that is, more intensely and with more frequency. In terms of theoretical approach, this program is rooted in ecological research, strategic planning, cognitive and social learning theory, and social skills intervention research based on those theories. In combining multiple frameworks, Stop & Think approaches social skill development from multiple research-validated perspectives.

The program is made up of five teaching and learning components: (1) teaching social skills in a step-by-step approach, (2) modeling the steps in real-world and relevant scenarios, (3) role-playing the steps to promote group participation in fun and engaging techniques, (4) performance feedback for constant support of students' successes and shortcomings, and (5) applying the skills to ensure maintenance and continuity. A classroom material set includes a teacher guide with reproducible resources and activities, 25 sets of cue cards, Stop & Think signs for creating behavior reminders throughout the classroom, and five posters for creating an environment of appropriate behavior awareness. As a whole unit, Stop & Think emphasizes social and emotional skills that fall under multiple interpretations of social competence we presented in Chapter 2.

Sample of Evidence Supporting Efficacy

Hall, J. D., Jones, C. H., & Claxton, A. F. (2008). Evaluation of the Stop & Think Social Skills Program with kindergarten students. *Journal of Applied School Psychology, 24,* 265–283.

The Tough Kid Social Skills Book

Author: Susan M. Sheridan, PhD

Publication Date: 2010

Publisher: Pacific Northwest Publishing

Website: *toughkid.com/series.html*

The premise behind The Tough Kid Social Skills Book is that students with "tough" reputations have difficulty in social situations largely because they have never been taught how to get along with others or behave appropriately in social situations. In this framework, social difficulties are viewed as a skill deficit more so than a processing problem. Therefore, this curriculum aims to help "tough" kids learn and maintain the skills and behaviors required for success in a variety of social and academic school situations.

Designed for use by teachers in grades 3–7, the program includes lessons on recognizing and expressing emotion, having conversations, joining a group, playing cooperatively, solving problems, using self-control, resolving arguments, dealing with teasing and being left out, and accepting "no" from peers and adults. The Tough Kid Social Skills Book is a school-based curriculum developed for structured use in small group, classroom, or whole-school application and to be used as either a stand-alone program or as a supplemental activity in a specific content area. Similar to other curricula described in this chapter, The Tough Kid Social Skills Book can be used as primary, secondary, or even tertiary social skills intervention.

The included curriculum guide supports teachers in identifying which students need additional social skills support, generating data for ongoing assessment of social skills levels, facilitating effective social skills learning opportunities, and becoming well versed in language, which fosters social and emotional growth. Multiple conceptualizations of social competence are represented in The Tough Kid Social Skills Book, including emotional and psychological competencies, "social knowledge," and school readiness skills.

Sample of Evidence Supporting Efficacy: Indirect

Crum, C. F. (2004). Using a cognitive-behavioral modification strategy to increase on-task behavior of a student with a behavior disorder. *Intervention in School and Clinic, 39*(5), 305–309.

DuPaul, G. J., & Weyandt, L. L. (2006). School-based intervention for children with attention deficit hyperactivity disorder: Effects on academic, social, and behavioural functioning. *International Journal of Disability, Development and Education, 53*(2), 161–176.

SUMMARY, CONCLUSION, AND WHAT'S AHEAD

In this chapter, we described the term *evidence based* as it pertains to education curricula and intervention programs. We presented ways in which curricula can be evaluated by the merit of its evidence base, why this merit is important, and how practitioners can determine whether a program in which they are interested is supported by evidence of efficacy. Also in this chapter, as a resource guide for teachers invested in classroom-based instruction aimed at improving students' social competence, we described many available social skills curricula. We believe this current chapter is helpful to teachers in elementary classroom settings who choose to address students' social competencies in a proactive and explicit manner.

Although frequently overlooked in favor of improving academic skills directly, instruction in social domains at the classroom level can—and should—be part of primary intervention efforts and is a viable pathway toward enhancing overall academic achievement. However, some students, particularly those with disabilities that affect their social competence, may need additional support, which can be provided through more intensive primary, secondary, and tertiary pedagogical choices designed to target specific social deficits. In Chapter 5, we present additional pedagogical approaches, such as peer-mediated instruction, which may prove to be effective for students who struggle with some packaged classroom curricula. Later, in Chapter 6, we offer methods for assessing the social competence needs of individual students, and in Chapter 7 we discuss components of individualized social skills intervention plans. The following is a summary list of major points covered in Chapter 4:

✓ Finding time to directly teach the skills associated with social competence can be challenging, but helping elementary students develop these skills is crucial to their long-term academic and social trajectory.

✓ Addressing the social skills of students with and without disabilities improves the school experiences of all students.

✓ Teachers who emphasize social competence with their instructional choices provide students with and without disabilities opportunities to learn social rules and expectations in safe and nurturing environments.

✓ For students with disabilities especially, fostering a classroom environment that emphasizes social competence in structured, instructional formats is particularly important, because it helps them to develop the social and emotional skills that many take for granted.

✓ In several instances, students with disabilities struggle to build and maintain authentic friendships with peers. Thus, addressing the skills involved in establishing peer relationships is essential to the social participation of students with disabilities.

✓ The use of evidence-based practices is important when providing effective social competence instruction.

✓ The gold standard method of evaluating the effectiveness of curricula is through empirical scientific research, published in a peer-reviewed outlet, which attests to the strength and overall benefit of the intervention or program.

✓ Many types of research methodology exist; however, experimental design which utilizes randomized control trials is considered the most sound and rigorous.

✓ When determining whether a curriculum or instructional program has merit, look for evidence of its effectiveness through (1) empirical research, (2) theoretical support, and (3) teacher testimonials.

CHAPTER 5

Capitalizing on the Power of Peers

In addition to targeting social skills through use of schoolwide programs and published curricula, another way that elementary school teachers can highlight social skills in their classrooms is by using peer-mediated instructional techniques as their approach to content instruction. In this chapter, we describe peer-mediated academic instructional strategies that have demonstrated efficacy for increasing both academic and social outcomes in inclusive elementary classrooms. We focus here on the use of cooperative learning groups, although other peer-mediated small-group instructional strategies, such as peer-tutoring dyads, can also foster social growth in elementary school classrooms.

Most teachers have experience placing their students in small groups for instruction. In a general education classroom, placing students into small groups is often a matter of practicality and logistics. Seasoned teachers also recognize that using small groups increases active engagement in the classroom and provides students with more opportunities to respond and practice new skills.

However, there is a continuum of benefits to small-group work, with some arrangements and activities being far superior to others. In this section we briefly describe the theoretical underpinnings that explain the positive impact that group work has on the social landscape of inclusive classrooms. We also summarize the benefits of various aspects of small-group instructional arrangements, paying attention to those aspects that enhance the development of all students' social and academic skills and, more specifically, the social acceptance and success of students with disabilities.

THEORETICAL RATIONALE

Teachers in general education classrooms use small groups for instruction for a variety of reasons, primarily related to the academic benefits of allowing students to learn from one another as they grapple with academic tasks. However, there are also ample social benefits that students experience when placed in heterogeneous groups for instruction.

Around the time of the start of the U.S. civil rights movement, Harvard psychologist Gordon Allport developed the contact theory of intergroup relations (1954). This theory holds that when people from different backgrounds work together on an equal footing to achieve common goals and get to know one another as individuals, they shed their prejudices and friendships may evolve. However, not all forms of small-group instruction provide a platform for students to work toward a common goal with equal opportunities for success. In fact, if constructed carelessly, some small-group tasks can create an environment in which stereotypes are reinforced and social relations are hindered. In this chapter, we highlight those aspects of small-group instruction that satisfy the requirements of Allport's contact theory and lay the groundwork for promoting positive, authentic peer relationships in the classroom.

It is important to note that Allport's theory was developed with the idea of improving interactions among individuals with different racial and ethnic identities in mind. Our focus here is on improving interactions among students with disabilities and their peers in general education classrooms. As we have pointed out in earlier chapters, students with disabilities are still less well accepted and more frequently rejected on sociometric measures than their peers without disabilities. Carefully planned small-group instructional activities have all the benefits of efficient instruction (e.g., increasing engagement and opportunities for students to practice new skills) with the additional benefit of having the potential to encourage the development of social skills and positive peer relationships.

COOPERATIVE LEARNING

Small-group instruction, as opposed to whole-class instruction, is an instructional arrangement wherein students within a class are divided into groups for the purpose of learning (Lou et al., 1996). Utilizing small-group instruction enables teachers to increase instructional time and increase opportunities for students to respond and practice new academic skills in ways that have been linked to higher outcomes for students with disabilities. Conversely, excessive reliance on whole-group instruction and individual seatwork sets the stage for off-task behavior by students who need more hands-on instructional guidance to be successful.

Another benefit of small-group instruction is that it increases a teacher's ability to individualize instruction, a necessary but challenging prospect for teachers who are charged with providing individualized attention or delivering "special education" in a large-group setting. With students working in small groups, teachers are free to give instructions or explanations to the whole class or just to specific groups. This arrangement also allows teachers to easily vary assignments or instructions within the larger group. The merit of this aspect of small-group instruction is punctuated by Lou et al.'s (1996) finding in their meta-analysis of group instruction that effect sizes were higher when teachers individualized instructional materials across groups.

In order to best capitalize on the strength of small-group instruction, educators should be mindful of four important elements:

1. Group composition.
2. Nature of the group task.
3. Individual accountability.
4. Relative ability of group members.

These four elements can have a significant impact on increases in task-related interactions and increases in academic achievement.

Group Composition

The decision to place students in heterogeneous versus homogeneous ability groups depends on the nature of the learning task (Noddings, 1989). With regard to subject area of instruction, a meta-analysis of within-class grouping found that overall effect sizes for homogeneous and heterogeneous ability instructional groups in mathematics and science were not significantly different; in reading, however, homogeneous ability groups were superior (Lou et al., 1996). This may be because tasks in math and science are typically more hierarchical; thus, discussion with and assistance from peers of varying abilities may be more likely to benefit student progress (Lou et al., 1996).

Lou et al.'s (1996) meta-analysis also determined that the effects of homogeneous versus heterogeneous groups were not stable across student ability. Students whose academic skills were low learned significantly more in heterogeneous groups, regardless of subject matter. This is most likely because low achievers have the most to gain from peer interaction around learning tasks. Low achievers in homogeneous groups lack models of more capable thinkers as well as peers who can stretch their learning by pushing the limits of their zones of proximal development.

The benefit of participating in learning tasks with peers of differing abilities applies to social learning as well. For students who exhibit challenging behavior, the social benefits of learning side by side with peers who are more socially adept are well established. This research underscores that the social and academic growth of students with disabilities is maximized by their participation in heterogeneous ability groups during small-group instruction, particularly in math and science. Also, if Allport's (1954) contact theory is applied to relations between students with disabilities and their peers without disabilities, small groups composed of students from both of these categories will produce increases in positive interactions between them.

Nature of the Group Task

Designing a cooperative learning lesson starts with learning objectives that are cooperative in nature or require interdependence to complete successfully. Simply placing students in groups and asking them to complete an assignment that could just as easily have been completed alone will not reap the positive social benefits that small group work has to offer.

Although it may seem obvious, one important part of designing a cooperative lesson to keep in mind is that the task must include a true group goal, otherwise known as *positive interdependence*. Positive interdependence exists when individual students perceive that their accomplishments contribute positively to the accomplishments of others. When students in small groups are recognized for the accomplishments of their group as a whole, positive interdependence is in place and the learning is considered cooperative. When students are physically placed into small groups for instruction but no structure is in place for positive interdependence, the learning is considered competitive or individualistic in nature. Students working toward a collaborative or group goal have been found to develop concepts that are richer and more precise than students who work independently under competitive or individualistic goal structures (Kol'tsova, 1978).

Ensuring that students work toward a group goal is best facilitated by assigning group tasks. A group task is one that requires some type of input from all the group members for the group to be successful (Cohen, 1994). A task that could easily be completed by the individual group members without each other's input or assistance is not likely to facilitate interaction for all group members. This is particularly true for low-ability or low-status students who may be perceived by their group mates as having little to offer or students who are rejected socially. To circumvent this problem, Cohen and Cohen (1991) suggest utilizing a classroom management system that encourages students to be responsible for each other's success, issuing specific roles during group work to help ensure that groups function in a prespecified manner and utilizing ill-structured tasks (i.e., ones that do not have a single correct answer) for group collaboration. Figure 5.1 presents sample cooperative learning group tasks and includes sample group tasks that lack some elements that encourage positive interdependence, along with suggestions on how to improve those tasks to optimize their effectiveness for promoting social competence and collaboration.

Positive interdependence in small-group work can be created through goal interdependence, as described previously, but can also be promoted through contingencies and reward structures. This is referred to as *reward interdependence*. An effective technique for teachers is to set up reward interdependence, creating a cooperative learning group task for which all group members receive a reward when the group collectively has met some standard. In behavioral literature, this concept is referred to as an interdependent group contingency. When an interdependent group contingency is set up, student group members will encourage each other to ensure that the group is successful. Instigating an interdependent group contingency has the added effect of ensuring that all group members actively participate and thus have the chance to benefit academically.

According to Slavin (1995), creating an interdependent group contingency is the best way to avoid small-group work in which one or more members "slack off" or where low-status or low-ability students are discouraged from participating. By making increased achievement the group goal for all members and by rewarding groups that accomplish their goal (i.e., reward interdependence), all members of a group will be

Following are sample small-group learning objectives for a cooperative lesson for a second-grade classroom.

SAMPLE 1: In groups of five, create a poster that shows the "who, what, when, where, and why" for *The Adventures of Taxi Dog* by Deb and Sal Barracca.

Problem: It is possible for a single student to do all the work.

Improvement: In groups of five, create a poster that shows the five "W's"—who, what, when, where, and why—for *The Adventures of Taxi Dog* by Deb and Sal Barracca. Each student should take one of the W words and create a draft of a picture that represents their W word. The final poster for each group should include a section from each of the group members.

Benefit: In this improved group task, it is necessary for all five group members to participate in order for the group to be successful.

SAMPLE 2: In pairs, review the spelling words in preparation for tomorrow's spelling test.

Problem: Neither student has any vested interest in their partner learning the spelling words.

Improvement: In pairs, take turns giving your partner a practice spelling test. Record how many words each partner gets right on the first practice test. Take turns giving practice tests until each partner improves by five words or gets a 100%.

Benefit: In this improved task, the pair does not successfully complete the task until both partners have made educational gains.

FIGURE 5.1. Group tasks that encourage positive interdependence.

more likely to interact, maximizing academic growth for all. Various researchers have supported this notion, reporting that the greatest effects of cooperative learning come when groups are rewarded for the increased achievement of all the members of their groups (Davidson, 1985; Ellis & Fouts, 1993; Manning & Lucking, 1991; Slavin, 1983). See Figure 5.2 for examples of interdependent group contingencies, based on a sample fourth-grade science lesson, that could be adapted for use in inclusive classrooms to promote cooperative behavior during small-group work.

Overall, positive interdependence that is established by utilizing group rewards in conjunction with group goals maximizes the positive effects of small-group instruction on academic growth for all students. Tudge (1992) contends that adding these factors to group work introduces the element of motivation that is lacking in most work in the Vygotskian and Piagetian traditions. He views this as a step in the direction of acknowledging that contextual factors also influence learning when peers come together around academic tasks.

As an example, how much two children's zones of proximal development overlap may not matter if they simply refuse to speak to each other. Explicit group goals and group rewards provide the motivation for the valuable interaction to take place. This distinction may be especially relevant for students with emotional or behavioral disorders, who are prime candidates for missing the benefits of task-related peer interaction if they are left in small groups with little structure and who traditionally have responded well to behavioral interventions.

Consider a sample cooperative learning group lesson for a fourth-grade science class, with the goal that students, in small groups, will record their collective hypotheses, conduct a buoyancy experiment using teacher-defined roles, and then record their observations on a group summary sheet.

Sample interdependent group contingencies to accompany this lesson:

- Students get a token for each observation they contribute to the summary sheet. Individual students cannot earn more than three tokens. At the end of the lesson, every group that has at least one token per group member gets to pick out their balloons from a box of specially decorated balloons to be used in the next experiment. (Groups that do not meet the minimum criterion of at least one token per group member will use plain balloons supplied by the teacher for the next experiment.)
- If a group can explain to the teacher how their recorded hypotheses reflect everyone's thinking, then that group's name gets listed on a Super Stars chart.
- When completing a group self-evaluation, if the group notes that everyone participated in conducting the experiment using their assigned roles, then all group members earn an "A" for participation for the day.

These example contingencies are interdependent because no one in the group gets the reward unless every member of the group accomplishes the goal.

FIGURE 5.2. Sample interdependent group contingencies.

Individual Accountability

While the importance of having all group members invested in their group mates' success has been established, it is also important to build in a mechanism for individual accountability. A lesson that includes individual accountability ensures that growth or success for each student in each group is given attention. Individual accountability is in place when the teacher overseeing the lesson can ascertain on an individual basis whether or not students have met the learning objectives. Examples of ways that individual accountability can be ensured include:

- Individual quizzes.
- Individual summary sheets submitted along with group summary sheets.
- Group lessons that require individual students to acquire expertise on a topic and share information on that topic with group mates in order to complete the group project.

In all these examples, a teacher could easily check an individual student's learning and hold each student accountable for mastering learning objectives.

Relative Ability of Group Members

As underscored earlier in the chapter, the relative abilities of the members of a group— both in academic as well as social domains—has a significant impact on the success of cooperative learning groups as a mode of instruction. Assuming an increase in the social acceptance of students with disabilities is a goal, the cooperative learning group tasks that teachers create must involve quality interactions. One important way to promote quality interaction is to ensure that all group members believe they have an equal opportunity for success. If tasks are structured in such a way that certain members of the group can succeed more easily than others, the stage for divisiveness may be set. Placing students in heterogeneous-ability cooperative learning groups will not necessarily lead to an increase in positive interactions unless some structure is built into the activity to create an "even playing field." Creating group tasks in which all students believe they can contribute to the good of the group helps promote acceptance and leads to more positive interactions and, it is hoped, to increased achievement.

Some specific manifestations of cooperative learning have these structures. For example, researchers at Johns Hopkins University have developed cooperative learning techniques that allow students to contribute to their group's goal by improving their own past performance. In these methods, group rewards are given to groups based on the extent to which individual members meet or exceed their own earlier levels of achievement. These methods prevent group members from viewing low-achieving students as burdensome and promote acceptance of students for whom mastery of academic content is more challenging, including some students with disabilities (Madden & Slavin, 1983; Slavin, 1984).

Because students with behavioral disorders and learning disabilities are typically low achievers, increases in positive peer interactions resulting from participation in cooperative learning groups should be maximized in methods that provide equal opportunities for success for all students. Increases in peer interactions should then lead to better understanding of the academic content around which the interactions take place.

To create cooperative learning activities that provide students with disabilities with equal opportunities for success, teachers sometimes have to be highly creative. When using a cooperative learning method such as Slavin's (1995) Student Teams Achievement Divisions, groups are rewarded for their joint performance on quizzes, but students add to their group's performance depending on how much they improve from their previous quiz score. This allows students to compete with themselves rather than feeling like they all must meet the same criteria to be deemed successful.

Other forms of cooperative learning produce equal opportunities for success by allowing for alternative forms of assessment or by using group projects that allow for multiple forms of contribution (e.g., one person draws, one acts out a concept, one summarizes) as assessment activities. In these ways, students are allowed to contribute according to their strengths while everyone is still held responsible for learning and demonstrating that learning.

SAMPLE COOPERATIVE LEARNING LESSON PLAN

Figure 5.3 provides an example of a lesson plan for a cooperative learning lesson designed to be used in an inclusive elementary classroom. Sample objectives for the whole class as well as for individual students with disabilities (i.e., student with "unique

Curriculum Areas: Social Studies, Language Arts, and Writing

Time Frame: 90 minutes

Name of Unit: The *Harris Burdick* books: Creating our own *Harris Burdick* stories

Lesson: "100% Smart" (Lesson 5 of 10)

Grade Level: 4/5

I. Major Concept Underpinning Lesson (Enduring Understandings/Essential Questions)

After the lesson, students will be able to discuss and describe:

a. The theory of multiple intelligences, including being able to describe each of the nine intelligences with language used in class.
b. Examples of each multiple intelligence.
c. Their own multiple intelligence strengths and weaknesses using Gardner's theory of multiple intelligences.
d. How each student is "100% Smart" and possesses at least some of each intelligence.
e. How each student's multiple intelligence strengths contribute to and help our community and classroom.

After the lesson, students will acknowledge that each student has different intelligences and will be able to use their multiple intelligence profile to compliment the profiles of others.

After the lesson, students will become more comfortable presenting in front of their peers. Students should also feel more comfortable in collaborative group work.

II. District Standards/Benchmarks Addressed in This Lesson

Local School District Social Studies Standards for Grades 4/5 (Example)

a. Students will develop a deeper understanding of themselves and the learning of others.
b. Students will listen to and comprehend oral communication.
c. Students will develop vocabulary of words or phrases to communicate in academic settings.
d. Students will recognize and use language appropriate to the context and situation.
e. Students will describe and prioritize personal skills and interests they want to develop.
f. Students will apply self-reflection techniques to recognize their strengths, weaknesses, and aspirations.

Local School District Language Arts Standards for Grades 4/5

g. Students will be able to identify and use parts of a book related to word meaning.
h. Students will be able to identify stated information about story elements.
i. Students will be able to analyze literary text.
   1. Make inferences about story elements.
   2. Draw conclusions.

(continued)

FIGURE 5.3. Sample cooperative learning lesson plan. Provided by Ms. Kari Steck, Madison, Wisconsin.

3. Analyze stated or implied theme or main idea.
4. Make inferences based on text features.

Local School District Writing Standards for Grades 4/5

j. Students will plan and write texts to entertain or explain.
k. Students will use real world authors as mentors.
l. Students will generate own ideas.
m. Students will use an effective strategy to plan for writing.
n. Students will use voice appropriate for the audience and purpose.
o. Students will reread own writing for clarity of message.
p. Students will give and receive appropriate feedback to support peer revision.

III. Lesson Objectives and Outcomes

After discussing students' "strongest smarts" and "growing smarts," and the benefits of using our smarts to improve the classroom community, students will be placed in a group of three to four based on complementary skills/intelligences. (Groups constructed in advance by teacher)

Students will be able to work together collaboratively while using their "strongest smarts" to create a story that follows the selected picture from *The Mysteries of Harris Burdick*.

IV. Lesson Objectives for Students with Unique Learning Needs

a. Kareem

Kareem will use his switches or items to make a choice between two items.

1. Kareem will reach toward item or turn towards item if it is wanted.
2. Kareem will use an All-Turn-It Spinner from Ablenet.com. He will hit a switch to activate the spinner that will select descriptive words that his group or all groups will use in their stories.

b. David

David will stay on task during group work.
David will cooperate with his group members.

c. Jayquan

Jayquan will work collaboratively together with his group members.

1. Jayquan will stay with the group.
2. Jayquan will listen to the ideas of his group members.
3. Jayquan will contribute at least one idea or agree to at least one of the ideas offered by another group member.

d. Trey

Trey will listen to the ideas of his group members.

Trey will contribute at least one idea or agree to at least one of the ideas offered by another group member.

(continued)

FIGURE 5.3. *(continued)*

e. Brian

Brian will present his ideas and thoughts to his group members clearly and in a voice loud enough to be easily understood by the other group members.

Brian will stay on task and use his self-monitoring chart as necessary.

V. Student Assessment Procedures (Evidence of Learning)

A. Student Stories

Students will be evaluated based on their performance during their group work time. Evaluation will be based on understanding of intelligences, participation and collaboration during planning time, and participation during the presentation of their group's story.

B. Student Evaluations

Students will evaluate their group members' performance of their roles in the group using the Grade Your Group Member form. Students will evaluate each individual group member, as well as themselves and the group as a whole.

1. Writer
   - Did the writer write clearly?
   - Did the writer listen to the group members' thoughts?
   - Did the writer write at least one page?

2. Idea-Maker/Motivator
   - Did the idea-maker stay focused?
   - Did the idea-maker motivate group members to participate?
   - Did the idea-maker develop key points to the story?

3. Presenter
   - Did the presenter accurately present the group story?
   - Did the presenter speak clearly and loudly?

VI. Previous Knowledge

a. Students must recall the nine intelligences taught in Lesson 1 (i.e., Linguistic, Interpersonal, Intrapersonal, Bodily–Kinesthetic, Naturalistic, Spatial, Musical, Logical–Mathematical, Existential). Posters will be available for groups to reference.

b. Students must know their strongest multiple intelligences and how they can help their group members by using this intelligence. Classroom bar graphs will be available for student reference.

VII. Multilevel and Multisensory Materials

a. Posters are available for students to reference, in addition to handouts describing the definitions of each intelligence and examples of each intelligence that were generated earlier by the class.

b. Pictures photocopied from the individual stories from *The Mysteries of Harris Burdick* by Chris Van Allsburg will be handed out in each group's packet to help students have a visual image of the story. Pictures will also serve as context clues for the stories.

(continued)

FIGURE 5.3. *(continued)*

VIII. Key or New Vocabulary/Concepts

Gardner's Multiple Intelligences: Linguistic, Interpersonal, Intrapersonal, Bodily–Kinesthetic, Naturalistic, Spatial, Musical, Logical–Mathematical, Existential.

IX. Teaching Procedure and Techniques (Estimated Time Frames for Each Component):

A. Introduction or Anchor Activity (4 minutes)
1. Recall Lesson 1. Hold up each poster for each multiple intelligence one at a time. Ask students to describe their thinking behind the descriptions posted under each multiple intelligence.
2. Recall Lesson 3 (bar graphs). Discuss ways we can help our classmates improve their smarts. Explain to the class that we'll be doing an activity to use our strong smarts to produce one group project. Essentially the project will be made from all of our class's smarts combined and will be 100% Smart!

B. Instructional Sequence (1 hour)
1. Pass out one drawing from *The Mysteries of Harris Burdick* to each student.
2. Ask students to develop a story to go with their interpretation of the book. Encourage students to edit their writing as a group.
3. Students will be expected to make up a short story by collaboratively using each other's ideas and thoughts. Assign student groups, with one student in each group being the Idea-Maker/Motivator, one being the Writer, and one being the Presenter. Tell students you assigned roles in each group based on each student's intelligences.
4. Explain that sometimes it takes more than one person to create a book, and that sometimes the result of combining intelligences is better than one intelligence on its own.
5. When student groups are finished with their stories, have each group present their story, with the Presenter reading the story aloud.

C. Closure (25 minutes)
1. Twenty-five years after he published *The Mysteries of Harris Burdick*, Chris Van Allsburg has put stories to the mysterious drawings of Harris Burdick. Van Allsburg has enlisted some of the most talented children's and adult's literature authors to write their own short stories based on his drawings.
2. Read stories from *The Chronicles of Harris Burdick* by Chris Van Allsburg: Jon Scieszka and Lemony Snicket
3. Compare the stories developed by the class to the stories developed by the authors. Explain to the class that while linguistic intelligence may not be one of everyone's strongest intelligences, sometimes our other intelligences influence our writing, making our linguistic intelligences stronger.
4. Ask students how they used their strongest intelligences to help members of their group.

D. Transition to Next Activity (1 minute)
1. Have students turn in finished stories to be compiled later into a class book.
2. Go to lunch.

(continued)

FIGURE 5.3. *(continued)*

X. Cooperative Learning Elements

    a. Positive interdependence
        1. To create a *Harris Burdick* story, students will be required to work together through their assigned roles as a group.
        2. Students will combine their individual strongest intelligences while working together within their groups to develop their *Harris Burdick* story.
    b. Individual accountability
        1. Each student will be assigned the role of either Writer, Idea Maker/Motivator, or Presenter.
        2. Students will evaluate their individual work in the group using the Grade Your Group Members form. (See Figure 5.4.)
    c. Group processing
        1. Each student will evaluate the participation of their group members using the Grade Your Group Members form.
        2. Each group member will evaluate how well their group worked together using the Grade Your Group Members form.
    d. Social skills
        Students will work together with peers they might not usually work with, strengthening the classroom community.
    e. Face-to-face interaction
        Students will be working together closely in small groups to create their *Harris Burdick* story.

XI. Extension/Enrichment

Students who have mastered the concepts of multiple intelligences can serve as mentors to students who are having a more difficult time.

Follow-Up/Alternate Activities:

- If the activity is not finished in the allocated 90-minute block, students will be allowed to finish after lunch during reading.
- Student groups who finish early can finish their "100% Smart" essays (assigned during a previous lesson).

XII. Application/Maintenance and Generalization of Skills/Concepts in Subsequent Lessons, Classes, or Curricular Areas

    a. Students will use their knowledge of multiple intelligences to learn how to better themselves as well as their community.
    b. Students will use their "strong smarts" to help other students improve these same skills.
    c. Students will be aware that we are all "100% Smart."

FIGURE 5.3. *(continued)*

learning needs") are provided. The lesson is tied to hypothetical school district standards for social studies, language arts, and writing for fourth and fifth grades. Example assessment activities are provided in Section V and the specific elements of the lesson that exemplify the cooperative element are highlighted in Section X of the sample lesson plan. A sample rubric that could be used to allow group members to self-assess their own as well as their peers' participation in the cooperative learning lesson is also provided as Figure 5.4. This self-assessment reinforces the positive interdependence incorporated into the lesson.

SUMMARY, CONCLUSION, AND WHAT'S AHEAD

In this chapter, we presented strategies for implementing one popular and effective form of peer-mediated instruction: cooperative learning groups. As discussed, it is important to remember that while teachers frequently utilize small-group learning techniques, there is a continuum of benefits associated with various forms of small-group work, with research demonstrating that some group strategies are more effective than others. When designing instruction that relies on group learning, teachers should consider the ways in which the individual needs of students can be met through peer mediation; it is certainly possible, but takes careful planning and organization. The following are

Grade Your Group Members		
Group Story Title: _____		
My Role: _____		
I feel that I: _____		
Writer: _____		
• Did the writer write clearly?	YES	NO
• Did the writer listen to the group members' thoughts?	YES	NO
• Did the writer write at least one page?	YES	NO
Idea Maker/Motivator: _____		
• Did the idea maker stay focused?	YES	NO
• Did the idea maker motivate group members to participate?	YES	NO
• Did the idea maker develop key points to the story?	YES	NO
Presenter: _____		
Did the presenter accurately present the group story?	YES	NO
Did the presenter speak clearly and loudly?	YES	NO

FIGURE 5.4. Cooperative learning lesson plan: Group member self-assessment. Provided by Ms. Kari Steck, Madison, Wisconsin.

important points for stakeholders in inclusive education to consider when designing peer-mediated instruction:

✓ Instructional methods that involve classmates working actively together increase student engagement in academic material, facilitate cooperation among peers, and create opportunities for friendships to develop between students with and without disabilities.

✓ As one supporting theory behind peer-mediated instruction, contact theory of intergroup relations (Allport, 1954) holds that when individuals from different backgrounds work together for a common cause and become acquainted with one another through the process of cooperation, they can shed their prejudices and friendships may evolve.

✓ While group instruction has many benefits, if implemented carelessly and without structure, it can actually hinder students' academic achievements and positive social interactions by creating an atmosphere of unequal student expectations and performance.

✓ For students with disabilities in inclusive classrooms, carefully planned small-group instructional activities facilitate opportunities to practice social competencies with their same-age peers in a safe and open environment.

✓ Relative to the education of students with disabilities, a substantial benefit to small-group instruction is that it increases teachers' ability to individualize instruction.

✓ In group work strategies, teachers may place students in either heterogeneous or homogeneous ability groups. Although each has potential benefits and drawbacks depending on the tasks at hand, mixed-ability groups facilitate positive interactions between students who may not be otherwise involved with one another and thus increases opportunities for friendships between students with and without disabilities.

✓ An important component of individual learning in group contexts is positive interdependence. This exists when individual students perceive that their accomplishments contribute positively to the accomplishments of others—a concept especially important for students with disabilities, because they may often struggle to see their contributions as worthwhile.

CHAPTER 6

Assessment of Individual Skills and Progress

with JENNIFER L. SCHROEDER

In these last two chapters, we finish our review of evidence-based practice with a focus on social development at the individual level. In Chapters 1 and 2, we established the importance of teaching social competencies to increase all students' chances for success in school. In Chapters 3 through 5, we reviewed approaches to promoting prosocial behaviors at the primary (Tier 1; schoolwide approaches) and secondary (Tier 2; classroom-level curricular interventions and peer-mediated instruction) intervention levels as a means of improving specific social skills in a way that leads to the development of long-term social competence. For some students (especially those in special education, who may have more significant and specialized needs), a more intensive, tertiary-level (Tier 3) intervention that matches each student's needs will be necessary to promote meaningful change. For these students, the only way to accomplish short-term goals related to successful development and utilization of social skills that will eventually lead to achieving the long-term goal of broader social competency is through an intervention plan that is both individualized and evidence based.

This individual intervention planning and implementation process includes four major activities: (1) assessment, (2) intervention development and implementation, (3) progress monitoring and evaluation of intervention effectiveness, and (4) planning for generalization and maintenance of skills. In this chapter, we focus on the assessment, progress monitoring, and evaluation of intervention effectiveness components that lead to the design and delivery of high-quality individual interventions for students with more severe or chronic social deficits.

Jennifer L. Schroeder, PhD, is Associate Professor in the Department of Psychology, Counseling, and Special Education at Texas A&M University–Commerce.

The meaning of *evidence based* at the tertiary level is both similar to and different from its definition at the primary and secondary levels. It is similar in that some individualized approaches to intervention (such as differential reinforcement) have sufficient research support to be considered evidence based, yet different because just knowing that an intervention is generally effective does not tell us if or how it will work for any individual child. Reliable and valid methods for conducting pre- and postintervention assessments are necessary for practitioners to determine whether they have chosen the right individual intervention. The student's individual characteristics, strengths, and weaknesses as well as both the school environment and the function of the problem behavior must be considered to identify the appropriate intervention for promoting social development. This is why tertiary-level interventions must begin with practitioners using high-quality, multicomponent assessment methods to evaluate the child, his or her environment, and the actions or reactions of other people. Therefore, individual assessment of the student and the environment and systematic implementation and monitoring of the interventions are the only way to evaluate if the chosen interventions are truly evidence based for each student.

When choosing assessment approaches for individual intervention plan development and evaluation, practitioners should evaluate evidence in the following areas: (1) reliability and validity of assessment measures for the purpose of identifying a student's social strengths and weaknesses; (2) quality of the assessment–intervention connection (does the assessment data collected lead us to make accurate decisions about which interventions will or will not be effective?); and (3) how schools will collect data to evaluate if the intervention is being implemented correctly and consistently (i.e., with integrity) and is effective at changing student behavior in the desired direction. To assist practitioners in making decisions about these various aspects of assessment, we present evidence relating to best practices in assessment as well as the strengths and weaknesses of various assessment approaches.

HOW TO ASSESS SOCIAL SKILLS AND WHAT TO MEASURE

At the tertiary level, it is important to remember that effective social skills intervention begins with an accurate assessment of the target student's current social skills set and an investigation into why he or she does not respond to initial intervention attempts. A thoughtfully developed, needs-based intervention that is aligned with the student's developmental level and current abilities is founded on an individual assessment that is both reliable[1] and valid.[2] Approaches to the assessment of social skills are similar

---

[1] *Reliability* refers to the consistency of measurement. Reliable assessment tools measure the same way across students and time. When thinking about reliability, imagine a scale for measuring a person's weight. It is only useful if it measures weight the same way regardless of the day it is used or the person who is standing on it. In this same way, reliable measurement of social skills should measure the skills the same way across students and time.

[2] *Validity* is the extent to which an assessment instrument (1) measures what it is supposed to measure, (2) has evidence to support the accuracy of interpretations made using the instrument, and (3) is used for a purpose consistent with the purpose for which the instrument was designed. Using the same

to assessment techniques used to evaluate academic, behavioral, and emotional functioning. Common techniques for identifying specific social skills needs and strengths typically include some combination of the following assessment techniques: review of student records, standardized rating scales, behavioral observation, interviews (student, teacher, parents, and, when appropriate, peers), and functional analysis of skills. In this age of data-based decision making, assessment options are plentiful. At times, the number of choices can be overwhelming, leading personnel to choose assessment options based on habit (what they were trained on or have regularly used), word of mouth (another professional told them it was useful), or an Internet search (a keyword search where we look at the first page or two and choose based on what looks good).

Although none of these are bad reasons for considering an assessment tool, the final decision as to which measure to use should be based on knowledge of all available options, best practices in assessment, and the needs of the individual student. In order to develop an individual intervention plan, we need to make individual choices about assessment. For example, the observation technique that gives us good data about one student may be unnecessary in the assessment of a different student's skills. Researchers in the field of social skills have identified the following features as being necessary for high-quality social skills assessment:

- Social skills assessment should begin at a global level (Elliott et al., 1989; Elliott & Busse, 1991). A first step for teachers or school teams is to review a student's overall social functioning, classroom expectations, and data on how the student responded to prior interventions (including universal and secondary interventions). This global review is typically completed by reviewing previous data collected regarding the student's skill strengths and weaknesses, meeting with the team to talk about the student's past performance, and having general discussions with the student's current and former teachers as well as with the parents.
- Multiple methods of social skills assessment should be used (e.g., Elliott et al., 1989; Elliott & Busse, 1991; Merrell, 2001; Sheridan & Walker, 1999). The use of multiple measures increases the validity of assessment results. It also allows for comprehensive data to be recorded across time, environments, and raters.
- Practitioners should use assessment tools that are psychometrically sound (i.e.,

---

analogy as reliability, a scale as an instrument of measurement is a valid measurement of weight (the purpose for which it was designed), but not a valid measurement of height. We know it is a valid measurement of weight because we have evidence to support its use and can check the interpretations we had (for example, we can use a different scale to check the accuracy of our measurement). Valid instruments for measuring social skills should (1) contain items that accurately represent the skill or set of skills they are trying to measure; (2) have scores that have evidence supporting their usefulness in describing, explaining, predicting, or changing a social skills; and (3) be used for the purpose for which they were designed (for example some instruments were designed to identify strengths and weaknesses while others were developed to measure change in skills over time). A final aspect of validity that is relevant to the measurement of social skills is social validity. When choosing a measure practitioners need to consider if the assessment instrument chosen is not just a good instrument, but is the right one for measuring the social skills of *this individual student*. For more information on aspects of validity and reliability see American Educational Research Association, American Psychological Association, and National Council on Measurement in Education (1999).

reliable and valid). If an assessment tool is not reliable and valid, then data from it will lead to erroneous conclusions.

- Practitioners should use assessment tools that are useful in practical settings. If it is not practically useful, then people will use it wrong, half-heartedly, or not at all, which leads to either bad data or no data at all.
- Practitioners should use assessment tools that have a clear link to intervention planning. The purpose of assessment in this case is not to make a diagnosis. An assessment tool that tells us a student has skills deficits or the depth of those deficits compared with a normative sample is not typically useful for intervention planning.

In this section on assessment tools, our purpose is to provide practitioners with (1) an overview of the best assessment tools available for conducting an individual evaluation of social skills, (2) a general description of the usefulness of each tool as well as its strengths and weaknesses, and (3) a summary of the research on how to best utilize these tools. The following are valuable resources for effective assessment.

Chafouleas, S., Riley-Tilman, T. C., & Sugai, G. (2007). *School-based behavioral assessment: Informing intervention and instruction.* New York: Guilford Press.—While this book does not focus specifically on social skills, it is helpful for practitioners looking for a user-friendly resource for conducting effective assessment that is useful for developing effective and efficient interventions. The book contains many case examples of applied strategies as well as reproducible checklists and forms.

Nangle, D. W., Hansen, D. J., Erdley, C. A., & Norton, P. J. (2009). *Practitioner's guide to empirically based measures of social skills (ABCT Clinical Assessment Series).* New York: Springer.—This book is one of the most comprehensive resources specifically related to the assessment of social skills. The editors cover social skills assessments for all ages (children through adults) and a wide variety of different types of mental illness (e.g., schizophrenia, autism). There are empirical reviews of all of the different approaches presented in this chapter, including information on the reliability and validity of different techniques. In addition, it includes a discussion of how to evaluate social skills at different stages of development. Practitioners will find this to be a useful resource in identifying potential evidence-based social skills-specific assessment tools that can be used as part of an individual student assessment.

STANDARDIZED RATING SCALES

Standardized rating scales provide practitioners with a quantitative summary of a student's social deficits or strengths across a variety of broad and specific domains of social competency. Most of these measures contain anywhere from 20 to 200 items that are rated using a Likert scale (typically a 3- to 5-point scale). These standardized scales tend to be norm referenced, meaning that the target student's score is compared with that of a normative sample of same-age or same-grade students. Norm-referenced rating scales are widely used to evaluate many types of behaviors in both students and adults. When using these types of tests, it is critical to choose tests that are psychometrically sound (i.e., documented reliability and validity and has a normative group that is current and representative). If the test is well constructed, most of the information a practitioner needs to evaluate the properties of the test can be found in the test manual. Additionally, practitioners can ask test publishers for research supporting the use of their measure. If research is available, most test publishers are eager to provide that information to potential customers. Of course, a quick literature search can also be done to evaluate recent research using the measure.

> A useful guide on how to find information
> on published tests can be found at
> *www.apa.org/science/programs/testing/find-tests.aspx.*

Rating scales used for social skills intervention planning can be categorized in two different ways: (1) either broad or narrow in scope and (2) a focus on students with a specific type of disorder or designed to measure skills regardless of other issues. Historically, the content of behavior rating scales focused on identifying the presence of specific types of problem behaviors or disorders. Current behavior scales have added items to the diagnostic items addressing areas related to social competency (e.g., social skills, aspects of motivation, leadership, engagement, cooperation, empathy, communication). These are identified generally as broad measures (multidomain) because they measure a wide variety of behavior domains, only one of which may be social skills. One example of a broad measure is the Behavior Assessment System for Children—Second Edition (BASC-2; Reynolds & Kamphaus, 2004). The BASC-2 can be used to identify the possible presence of a wide variety of different disorders (e.g., depression, anxiety, attention problems), but it also includes scales such as leadership, social skills, functional communication, negative emotionality, anger control, emotional self-control, and resiliency. Narrow measures (single domain) focus solely on different aspects of social competency. One example is the Social Skills Improvement System Rating System (SSIS; Gresham & Elliott, 2008). The entire focus of the SSIS is to identify various areas of social skills and skill deficits.

Deciding which scales, or what combination, to use for measuring a student's skills should be tied to the questions you want to answer with your assessment. Additional considerations for choosing an assessment should include, for example, rating format (pencil-and-paper format vs. computer based), rater options (self, parent, teacher), and link to intervention (some measures such as the SSIS offer companion intervention guides to help practitioners link assessment results to intervention choices). The following is a list of commonly used standardized rating scales that focus all or in part on assessment of social skills or social competency. See Table 6.1 for measure details, including scale type, raters, scoring options, age ranges, and ancillary materials. The measures listed next and in Table 6.1 are for use with all types of students, because they do not focus on any specific type of disability.

TABLE 6.1. Social Competence Rating Scales

Title and publisher	Scales	Raters and age range	Languages available	Scoring options	Administration format	Other
Academic Competence Evaluation Scales; Pearson Assessment	*Teacher Record Form:* Academic Skills Subscales: Reading/ Language Arts, Math, Critical Thinking Academic Enablers Subscales: Academic Motivation, Interpersonal Skills, Study Skills, and Classroom Engagement	Teacher Record Forms (grades K–12), Student forms (6–12), and College forms	English	Additional software is available for purchase to provide a scored summary report	Pencil and paper, administered to individual students	The *Academic Intervention Monitoring System* is a companion guidebook available to help implement intervention strategies There are also *AIMS Forms* available to identify the specific teaching and learning tactics used by students, parents, and teachers
Behavior Assessment System for Children, Second Edition (BASC-2); Pearson Assessment	*Teacher and Parent Scales:* Clinical Scales (e.g., anxiety) Adaptive Scales (e.g., activities of daily living) *Child Self-Report Scale:* Self-Report of Personality (e.g., attention problems, attitude toward school)	Parent and teacher (ages 2–21 years and 11 months), self-report (6 years–college age)	English, Spanish	Hand scored or computer scored with BASC-2 ASSIST to meet basic scoring needs or BASC-2 ASSIST PLUS for comprehensive scoring	Pencil and paper, administered to individual students	This test is designed to measure both behavioral strengths and problems, particularly internalizing and externalizing problems, school problems, and adaptive skills

Instrument	Content/Subscales	Raters/Ages	Language	Scoring	Administration	Notes
Behavioral and Emotional Rating Scale, Second Edition; PRO-ED	Interpersonal strength, involvement with family, intrapersonal strength, school functioning, affective strength, and career strength	Parents, teachers, or self-report (ages 5–18)	English, Spanish	Hand scored; summary reports are available from publisher	Pencil and paper; administered by teachers, parents, other school personal, or even self-report; administration time, approx. 10 minutes per student	Focuses only on the student's personal strengths and competencies
Devereux Student Strengths Assessment; Devereux Center for Resilient Children	*Social–Emotional Competencies Scales:* Self-Awareness, Social-Awareness, Self-Management, Goal-Directed Behavior, Relationship Skills, Personal Responsibility, Decision Making, Optimistic Thinking	Teachers or other school staff and parents/guardians; for use with elementary and middle school students	English	Hand scored using accompanying manual	Paper and pencil; form can be read aloud to raters with literacy problems or those who are learning English	The scale is designed to assess socioemotional competencies that serve as protective factors for children K–8. Since the scale is based on the student's strengths, it measures positive behaviors instead of maladaptive ones
School Social Behavior Scales, Second Edition (SSBS-2); Assessment-Intervention Resources	*Social Competence Scale:* Peer Relations, Self-Management/Compliance, and Academic Behavior. *Antisocial Behavior Scale:* Hostile/Defiant, etc.	Teachers or other school personnel; appropriate for students ages 5–18	English	Hand scored using the SSBS-2 manual	Pencil and paper; can be administered individually or in a group setting; typically lasting approx. 10 minutes per student	Designed to screen, assess, and plan interventions for children and youth with social competence and antisocial behavior problems

(continued)

TABLE 6.1. (Continued)

Title and publisher	Scales	Raters and age range	Languages available	Scoring options	Administration format	Other
School Social Skills Rating Scale; Slosson Educational Publications	Four school-related social behaviors scales: (1) Adult Relations, (2) Peer Relations, (3) School Rules, (4) Classroom Behaviors	Each individual scale is available for use at the elementary level. They are recommended to be administered by school personnel, specifically classroom teachers	English	Hand scored through use of accompanied manual	Pencil and paper; individual	Recommended specifically to special educators as a method for monitoring social IEP goals
Social Behavior Assessment Inventory; Psychological Assessment Resources	Curriculum-based rating instrument that measures performance of social behaviors in a classroom setting. Scales: Environmental Behavior, Interpersonal Behaviors, Self-Related Behaviors, and Task-Related Behaviors	Individual who has observed the child's social skills (teacher, parent, counselor, psychologist); grade range: K–9	English	Hand scored using accompanying manual	Paper and pencil; administered at the individual level	Program authors encourage use of resulting data for developing instructional approaches to social competence development
Social Emotional Assets and Resilience Scales; Psychological Assessment Resources	Scales measure the following areas of social-emotional competence: (1) Responsibility, (2) Self-Regulation, (3) Social Competence, (4) Empathy	Includes self-report measure for students in grades 3–6, self-report measure for students in grades 7–12, teacher report rating scale, parent report rating scale	English	Hand scored; programs for creating computer generated score reports, progress monitoring reports, and integrated score reports are available	Pencil and paper and computer based; individual	Is a strength-based approach to measuring social competence; focuses on what students do well

Instrument	Domains	Population	Languages	Scoring	Administration	Notes
Social Skills Improvement System (SSIS); Pearson Assessment	*Social Skills:* Communication, Cooperation, Assertion, Empathy, Responsibility, Engagement, Self-Control *Competing Problem Behaviors:*: Externalizing, Bullying, Hyperactivity/Inattention, Internalizing, Autism Spectrum *Academic Competence:* Reading Achievement, Math Achievement, Motivation to Learn	Includes parent rater forms for youth ages 3–18, teacher rater forms for the same age group and student self-report form for ages 8–12 and 13–18.	English, Spanish	Hand scored and computer scored (which includes multirater report generation option); will generate report with intervention suggestions	Pencil and paper and computer web based; includes audio CD to address students or parents with low reading skills; administered to individual students	Included are consent forms, parent letters, and teaching materials (cue cards, video clips) Its Class-Wide Intervention Program (CIP) contains lessons that are directly connected to skills assessed on the SSIS. The CIP focuses on 10 core skills, with each skill divided into three 25- to 20-minute lessons.
Walker–McConnell Scale for Social Competence and School Adjustment; Wadsworth	*Elementary version:* Teacher-Preferred Social Behavior, Peer-Preferred Social Behavior, and School Adjustment Behavior *Adolescent version:* Teacher-Preferred Social Behavior, Peer-Preferred Social Behavior, School Adjustment Behavior, and Social Adjustment and Empathy	Elementary (grades K–6) and middle and high school (7–12) teachers	English, Spanish	Hand scored using accompanying manual	Paper and pencil; administered at the individual level; duration of assessment approx. 10 minutes	Includes a technical manual, which explains research procedures for validating use of this scale.

Narrow scales focused on social skills:

- *Social Skills Improvement System Rating Scales* (SSIS; Gresham & Elliott, 2008). This is the updated and revised version of the original Skills Rating System (Gresham & Elliott, 1990). It allows for the assessment of social skills, problem behaviors, and academic competence in individual students.
- *School Social Behavior Scales—Second Edition* (SSBS-2; Merrell, 2002). These scales allow for a school-based assessment of social skills and antisocial behaviors in children and adolescents.
- *Social Emotional Assets and Resilience Scales* (SEARS; Merrell, 2011). This measure focuses on whether individuals possess certain social emotional assets such as empathy and social competence.
- *Devereux Student Strengths Assessment* (DESSA; LeBuffe, Shapiro, & Naglieri, 2009). This measure, as with the previous measure, focuses on positive attributes of social competence, such as self-management, viewing them as assets that children and adolescents may possess.
- *School Social Skills Rating Scale* (Brown, Black, & Downs, 1984). This scale helps school practitioners (e.g., classroom teachers and school psychologists) identify which social skills students struggle with the most, and from there offer a template on which to base an individualized behavior plan. It is a 40-item scale that locates social deficits, rather than strengths, thus providing data about specific areas that need to be targeted by intervention.

For more information on options for and measurement properties of these and other specific scales for rating social behaviors, see Humphrey et al. (2011).

The following broad scales include at least one socially related scale:

- *Behavior Assessment System for Children—Second Edition* (BASC-2; Reynolds & Kamphaus, 2004).
- *Behavioral and Emotional Rating Scale—Second Edition* (BERS-2; Epstein & Sharma, 2004).
- *Academic Competence Evaluation Scales* (ACES; DiPerna & Elliott, 2000) and *Academic Intervention Monitoring System* (AIMS; Elliott, DiPerna, & Shapiro, 2001).

Following are two additional assessment tools that are often cited in social skills literature and have been generally well reviewed, though current publication information is not readily available.

- *Social Behavior Assessment Inventory* (SBAI; Stephens & Arnold, 1992). This measure has been previously listed as being published by Psychological Assessment Recourses (PAR) but is no longer listed on their website.
- *Walker–McConnell Scale for Social Competence and School Adjustment* (SSCSA; Walker & McConnell, 1995). The adolescent version is still published by Cengage/Wadsworth, but not the elementary edition. The social skills companion guide for this measure is still available through ProEd (The Walker Social Skills Curriculum—The ACCEPTS Program, Curriculum Guide).

Because social skills are a central part of autism and other developmental disorders, scales that are designed to evaluate these disorders include social skills scales or solely focus on the assessment of social skills in this particular population. The benefit of using a disorder-specific scale is that they typically contain what are known as clinical norms.[3] In the case of autism, that would mean that the norms used to achieve a score included students with autism. It can be beneficial to compare a student with other students with a particular disorder rather than just typically developing students. Using both clinical and regular norms can give practitioners two different, yet useful, pictures of a student's strengths and weaknesses. Listed next are some social skills rating scales that have been specifically designed for students with autism:

- *Social Skills Checklist* (Quill, 2000). This checklist documents student acquisition (i.e., yes or no) of certain social behaviors in school and in community-related contexts, including play skills, group skills, and community social skills.
- *Social Responsiveness Scale* (SRS; Constantino & Gruber, 2005). This 65-item Likert (4-point) scale measures ASD response symptoms in areas related to social awareness, information processing, and anxiety.
- *Profile of Social Difficulty* (POSD; Coucouvanis, 2005). This 6-point Likert scale identifies domains of social difficulty in the context of fundamental skills, social initiation and response skills, and getting along with others skills.
- *Autism Social Skills Profile* (ASSP; Bellini, 2006). This comprehensive 4-point, 49-item scale profiles the social functioning of students with ASD. Social participation and social avoidance are of particular focus.

Benefits of Standardized Rating Scales

The benefits of standardized rating scales are many. First, they are easy to use and not time consuming (Merrell, 2000). Many times a rating scale can be completed in 10 to 15 minutes, with the rater receiving no more than brief instructions or support. They also require little expert training to administer. A second benefit is that most scales have separate forms for parents, teachers, and students of different ages (Merrell, 2000). These multirater options can be useful in helping a practitioner see the big picture and to collect information about low-frequency behaviors that are difficult, if not impossible, to observe.

A third benefit identified by Merrell (2000) is that they are more objective and reliable than some other measures of data collection. Rating scales are objective in that they have respondents evaluate statements that are carefully constructed using a clear, quantifiable rating. They can also be viewed as subjective in that they represent the rater's perception of the child, which may more or less reflect the child's behavior at any given time or in any particular environment. The increase in reliability over other methods is also not always clear. It is true that published rating scales typically have well-documented reliability (they consistently produce the same scores). Other methods in

---

[3]It should be noted that the BASC-2 also contains clinic norms (as well as separate norms by gender and age); these norms include students who were identified by their parents as having some type of clinical diagnosis. This clinical sample includes the diagnoses from participating students whose diagnoses run nearly the full range of special education categories (intellectual, developmental, learning, and emotional/behavior difficulties).

this chapter (observations and interviews) also have a high degree of reliability when those measures are structured and used by well-trained practitioners.

Often, several forms of one rating scale are utilized so that observations across settings can be capitalized upon (Merrell, 2000). For example, teachers and other school professionals complete a school-based or teacher version of a scale, and parents or guardians complete a home-based version of the same scale. Thus, teachers and other educational or medical professionals as well as parents and guardians are able to provide input about a student's behavioral performance in more than one context. Thus, behaviors can be compared across settings and forms can be completed by people who know the history of the behavior (Merrell, 2000).

It should be noted that at times the results from multiple raters can vary. These differences should not be interpreted as a failing of reliability or a respondent being untruthful. If the parents and teacher see different things, that is okay. Parents and teachers have different types of relationships and interactions with the student, so it would make sense that they would rate the behavior in different ways. When analyzing rating scale data, it is important to remember that each scale reflects that person's opinions and experiences. Because we all have different experiences and knowledge related to student behavior, it only makes sense that we would rate that behavior in different ways. In sum, because of the comprehensive nature and research-based advancement of behavioral rating scales, they deliver a macro-level analysis of students' behavioral capacity and intervention needs by people who are "experts" in the student's behavior (Merrell, 2000).

Limitations of Standardized Rating Scales

Although there are many benefits of using behavior rating scales during the assessment process, there are also drawbacks. First, behavior rating scales can be expensive. Thus, in an educational climate of limited resources, some schools may not have access to multiple rating scale options, leading people to use the scales they own rather than the appropriate scale to measure the behavior of a particular student. Additionally, while they may be relatively easy to administer, they still may require specialized training to score and interpret accurately. Because behavior rating scales appear simple, the specialized training may be easy to overlook. Schools may try to save money by having professionals not trained in the subtleties of interpretation write a report using the printout from a computer-generated report. Computers can report numbers and make suggestions based on those numbers, but they are no substitute for expert judgment.

Additionally, many of the rating categories are static, allowing for little to no flexibility when using rating scales. This means that behavior scales are limited in the complexity of information they can provide; the behaviors rated are explicit, and there is minimal room for negation if a social behavior witnessed is absent from the scale. Finally, rating scales may have limited sensitivity to change. The purpose of many rating scales is to identify the presence or absence of a disorder, not to evaluate change over time. They, therefore, may not be sensitive to detect small, gradual changes in behavior. When choosing a rating scale, practitioners should review the test manual to see if it is mainly useful for only the initial assessment of behavior levels or if it can also be used to evaluate change over time. Some measures, like the BASC-2, SSIS, or ACES, have been designed with progress-monitoring options.

OBSERVATIONS

Observation of social competence is, simply stated, the process of observing a student's social behaviors. Behavior observations can take place in the student's natural environment or in structured, practitioner-designed situations. Observations in both natural and artificial settings can be useful for understanding different aspects of a student's social needs and deficits. In addition to the student's behavior, aspects of the environment and the behaviors of others can be documented using observational techniques. This combination of information about student behaviors, the actions of other people, and the environment in which the behaviors happen provide rich information that can be used to both inform understanding of current behavior and assist in intervention development. In this section, we describe best practices in conducting observational assessments, types of observation settings, and the benefits and limitations of observational assessments. Although there are many books available on behavior observation, we have found the following resource to be particularly user-friendly for teachers and other school personnel who have not had formal training in observational assessment. It is short, focused, and has many graphs and examples.

Van Houten, R., & Hall, R. V. (2001). *The measurement of behavior: Behavior modification.* Austin, TX: Pro-Ed.

Behavior Observation Procedures

Although there are many different approaches that can be used effectively to collect observational data on social skills, there are certain core principles and procedures that affect the reliability and validity of measurement. Consideration of these principles and procedures, therefore, is at the center of any high-quality observational assessment. For the purpose of this chapter, we have identified six main steps for conducting an observation of behavior, and three additional considerations related to observation setting, benefits of observations techniques, and the limitations of observational approaches.

Step 1: Identify and Define the Behavior or Behaviors[4] That Will Be Observed

To conduct a meaningful observation of behavior, practitioners should start by developing an operational definition that can be used reliability by all members of the student's intervention team, including school staff, parents, and possibly the student. Good behavior definitions are to be observable and measurable. The measurable dimensions of behavior include (1) topography (what the behavior looks like); (2) intensity (i.e., mild, moderate, or severe); (3) temporal characteristics (i.e., how long a behavior lasts or how long it takes a student to respond to a command); and (4) valence (i.e., what are the positive and negative aspects of the behavior, and which of those aspects should be the focus of the observation?).

---

[4]Observers who decide to measure multiple behaviors at once need to make sure the method of recording data is structured so that keeping track of multiple behaviors is feasible and can be done accurately.

When developing a behavior definition, practitioners should start with information from parent and teacher reports of the behavior as well as commonly recognized components of a behavior. A trial observation where no data are collected can then be used to refine the definition to reflect behaviors that teachers or parents may not be aware of. Finally, a draft of the definition can be circulated so that everyone who will be observing can provide feedback for a final definition that will be used in both initial and progress monitoring observations.

When considering which behaviors will be observed, there are several behaviors that should be included in order to get a good picture of a student's social skills. Two behaviors to evaluate are social initiation and social responses. When evaluating a student's social skills, it is useful to know how often a target student *initiates* social interaction with peers and how the student *responds* to peers. These same behaviors should also be observed for peers and adults who interact with the target child during the observation period. That is, how do others initiate interactions and respond to initiations? When defining initiation and response, practitioners need to carefully consider how to define the differences among appropriate, inappropriate, and inconsistent behaviors. If initiation is measured as each time a student approaches another person, is the first one to speak, and the person responds, then an interaction where a student approaches a peer, says "Hi" in a whisper that is barely audible, and the peer says "What do you want?" would be recorded as an instance of initiation. In addition to initiation, response, and some of the traditional problem behaviors, practitioners may want to consider observing the presence or absence of the following behaviors: use of humor, ability to respond to nonverbal cues and other's use of abstract language, questions asked about topics outside of a student's area of interest, communication (e.g., verbal, nonverbal, pragmatics), cooperation, self-control/inhibition, respect, flexibility (shifting between tasks), use of prosocial skills, and engagement/sustaining behaviors over time.

Step 2: Determine How the Behavior Will Be Observed

It is critical for the observer to choose the technique that is an appropriate match for the type of behavior being observed. There are five common recording procedures used during observational assessments. The technique chosen should be the one that best records the behavior in order to document important aspects such as frequency, strength, duration, and intensity.

NARRATIVE RECORDINGS

This recording technique involves writing down a qualitative description of the observed behaviors. For narrative recordings to be useful in an individual assessment, they have to have some structure and a clear focus: Specific behaviors and certain aspects of behavior are identified at the outset. In contrast, with an unstructured approach, the observer just writes down whatever he or she sees. Unless the observation is being recorded, it will be impossible to write down everything that is happening. Therefore, without the structure of identifying specific aspects to look for in the observation, something is likely to be missed. For example, using a structured narrative, the observer may decide he or she wants to describe the language used every time a student initiates a social interaction; this compares with an unstructured observation where the observer tries to describe every aspect of every social interaction the student engages in. Multiple structured narratives can be conducted to better describe what different skills look like for an individual student. The data collected with these structured narratives can be used to develop observable and measurable operational definitions that can be applied when employing other specific observation techniques, listed below.

ABC RECORDING

This structured narrative recording involves documenting antecedent–behavior–consequence (ABC) sequences. ABC recording allows practitioners to document narrative data about what happens before and after the different behaviors and can be used as an initial observation technique to gather more information about the behavior of interest. These data can be useful in both identifying the function of a behavior and in intervention planning.

EVENT RECORDING

Event recording is used to document the frequency of a specific behavior. In event recording, the observer typically records a tally mark each time he or she observes the target behavior during the observation session. Event recordings are best used for behaviors with a clear beginning and end that neither occur too quickly nor last too long. It should be used when the number of times a behavior occurs, not how long the behavior lasts, is of primary concern. Event recording would work well, for example, to document the number of times a student initiated a conversation during a specified time period. It would not, on the other hand, be an appropriate technique if we were interested in how long a student engaged in conversation with others. See Figure 6.1 for an example of an event recording data sheet.

DURATION RECORDING

Duration recording involves documenting how long each instance of a behavior lasts. The practitioner typically records the start and stop times of a target behavior, for example, how long each of a student's social interactions lasts. In this example, duration (i.e., how long a conversation lasts) would be preferable to a frequency count (e.g., recording the number of words a student says during a conversation).

LATENCY RECORDING

Latency recording is used to document time between an antecedent (i.e., the student is greeted by a teacher) and the start of the corresponding behavior (i.e., the student responds to the teacher with an appropriate greeting). This is a useful measure of

Directions: Use a tally mark to record every time the target student engages in the targeted behavior.

Date of Observation: _____ Activity: _____

Operational Definition of Targeted Behavior: _____

_____

_____

_____

| | Time | | Notations of Occurrence | Total |
Date	Start	Stop		Occurrences

FIGURE 6.1. Event recording data sheet.

behavior when the interest lies in how long it takes a student to respond, and it is relatively easy to use.

INTERVAL RECORDING

Interval recording requires separating the observational sequence into time intervals and then documenting specific behaviors displayed during either all (whole-interval recording) or part (partial-interval recording) of the interval. Examples of behaviors that can be observed using interval recording include being engaged in conversation and cooperating with others. See Figure 6.2 for an example of an interval recording data sheet.

MOMENTARY TIME SAMPLING RECORDING

As with interval recording, momentary time sampling involves separating the observational sequence into intervals. However, in momentary time sampling, the presence or absence of specific behaviors at the end of each interval is recorded. It is important to note, however, that momentary time sampling will provide only a rough estimate of how often a behavior occurs.

FUNCTIONAL ASSESSMENT OBSERVATIONS

There are a variety of forms that allow raters to identify specific behaviors, their antecedents, and their perceived functions. Functional assessment observations (FAOs) differ from ABC recordings. FAOs use a checklist approach (quantitative) to identifying the presence or absence of a behavior or condition, whereas ABC recordings use a narrative (qualitative) description of what happens during each stage of the ABC sequence. For a complete description of FAOs and sample charts, see O'Neill et al. (1997).

CHOOSING AN OBSERVATION TECHNIQUE

For data being collected by an independent observer, interval techniques are preferable because they provide an accurate representation of a child's behavior across an observation period. Interval techniques, however, are not practical for use by classroom teachers because they require the observer to watch consistently for the entire observation period. For teachers collecting initial assessment or progress-monitoring data, either latency or momentary time sampling techniques are much more user friendly. For a thorough discussion of strengths and weaknesses of each technique as well as additional details on developing behavior definitions and observation procedures, see Skinner, Rhymer, and McDaniel (2000).

Step 3: Identify How the Observed Behavior Will Be Documented

Three options for documenting observation exist: (1) use a computer program (e.g., Word, Excel) to design your own behavior observation form, (2) use a published standardized

In each 30-second interval, record with a tally mark if the target student engages in one of the targeted behaviors.

Date of Observation: _____ Activity: _____

Behavior 1: _____

Behavior 2: _____

Behavior 3: _____

Interval	Behavior 1	Behavior 2	Behavior 3
30"			
1'			
1'30"			
2'			
2'30"			
3'			
3'30"			
4'			
4'30"			
5'			
5'30"			
6'			
6'30"			
7'			
7'30"			
8'			
8'30"			
9'			
9'30"			
10'			
10'30"			
11'			
11'30"			
12'			
12'30"			
13'			
13'30"			
14'			
14'30"			
15'			

FIGURE 6.2. Interval recording data sheet.

observation form, or (3) use electronic means to collect your data. Developing your own forms can initially be time consuming, because it can take several episodes of trial and error before you construct a form that is the right match for the behavior you are measuring. Once an initial template has been developed, however, it is cost effective and allows for great flexibility.

Using published measures can be easier because they often come with predeveloped definitions and set observation intervals. One example of a published measure is the Student Observation System (SOS; a companion measurement option for the BASC-2; Reynolds & Kamphaus, 2004). For practitioners who do not do these types of observations often or do not have strong computer skills, standardized forms may be a good option. Additionally, standardized forms can help ensure that everyone across a school district is collecting observation data in the same way, promoting consistency in ratings across environments and raters.

The final option for documenting observation involves using a computer, PDA, or tablet. Some published measures have computerized data collection forms available. For example, the BASC-2 Portable Observation System (Reynolds & Kamphaus, 2004), allows practitioners to create custom forms to collect observation data on both positive and negative behaviors. Newer electronic options include programs for PDAs or tablets (e.g., iPad, Android). Appendix 6.1 at the end of the chapter includes a description of current tablet applications that practitioners may find useful for conducting behavior observations. Electronic options allow for, among other benefits, ease of data entry (including electronic reminders for when to observe and record behaviors) and greater accuracy, because data are entered directly into electronic format; easy analysis (i.e., automatic graphing tools or option to export to a statistical program); and easy maintenance of data (ability to store multiple electronic files over time). Weaknesses of electronic programs include (1) potential risks to confidentiality if the data are not appropriately protected or if the electronic device is lost and (2) finding a program that is designed to match the type of data collection techniques you want to use. Four factors that practitioners should take into consideration when choosing a program are as follows: Can the program be customized? How many behaviors can be observed? Are there options to observe multiple students (in order to conduct peer comparisons)? What kind of security features are available to protect the data?

Step 4: Decide Who Will Observe as Well as When and Where He or She Will Observe

Although behavior observations are often conducted by school psychologists or behavior consultants, teachers and students themselves can serve as observers. When nonexperts are conducting the ratings, the complexity of procedures and number of observations are typically pared down, but the basic procedures remain the same. Just as multiple raters can provide rich data when using rating scales, observations conducted by multiple raters can provide a rich picture of a student's social skills. The difference with observation is that it is far more time consuming to train multiple raters to conduct multiple behavior observations. Observers should collect data at times and places where the behavior of interest is most likely to occur.

Step 5: Conduct Multiple Observations across Settings and Contexts

Multiple observations provide more accurate and comprehensive social skills data. Regarding the duration of an observation period, in order for data to be reliable, several observations in each setting or context are needed to ensure accurate assessment of behavior (Doll & Elliott, 1994). Thus, conducting an effective observational assessment necessitates substantial time commitments from trained observers, who are available to conduct multiple observations in different settings.

Step 6: Analyzing and Reporting the Observational Data

There are a variety of methods for analyzing observational data. Percentages can be calculated to evaluate how often the behavior occurred during the observation. The level of behavior can be compared with a socially valid standard (i.e., the teacher thinks that students should raise their hands every time they speak; in this case then, even one instance of calling out may be too much for this teacher). Levels of behavior can also be compared with peers. It is not uncommon for observers to include a comparison peer when collecting data. Comparison peers can be useful in evaluating if it is really a child-specific problem or possibly something broader that is happening in the classroom. A caution with interpreting peer comparison data: If a peer is chosen at random, there is no way to know if the peer's behavior is good or bad. Anyone who has conducted behavior observations has found themselves in a place where they realize they chose a peer who is not at all representative of average classroom behavior. A final method for evaluating observation data is to plot the data on a graph or scatter plot in order to evaluate the trends.

Types of Observational Settings

Behavior can be observed either in natural environments (e.g., classroom, playground, the student's home) or in constructed settings (i.e., a situation where the student has known problems or that tests the limits of his or her skills). Naturalistic behavior observation (NBO) takes place in a student's natural environment. For elementary school-age students, this could include classroom environments, recess, hallways, lunch, the bus, and, when appropriate, home or community settings. Researchers have identified central mechanisms for the usefulness of observational assessments. Observers must (1) be trained in specific observation techniques; (2) be objective; (3) use systematic, operational definitions/descriptions of behavior; and (4) conduct reliability checks to ensure the observation is being applied accurately and consistently (Jones, Reid, & Patterson, 1979; Merrell, 2001).

Natural Settings

The strength of naturalistic observations of social competence is that when behaviors are analyzed in the environment where they organically take place, the validity of the assessment data is increased (Elliott & Gresham, 1987). The increased validity of natural observation comes from being able to evaluate social skills in the natural contexts in which they occur. Recess and lunch periods, especially at the elementary level, are considered optimal for NBO because of the absence of structure and formality and the free-form nature of peer interactions at these times, (Merrell, 1999). Although other forms of behavioral observation exist (e.g., simulated laboratory observation), it can be argued that the most socially valid or authentic data come from NBO, because behaviors are being observed in the normal course of the student's activities. In the case of assessing social competency and planning for effective interventions, social validity is crucial.

Analogue Settings

While natural contexts are necessary for understanding a student's social skills, there are limits to what can be observed by just watching a student go through his or her day. For example, if we fail to see a student initiate appropriate interactions with peers in the classroom, we cannot determine if it is a skill acquisition deficit (the student does not know how to do it), performance deficit (the student has the skill but is not using it), fluency deficit (the performance is inconsistent), or performance is being affected by some competing motivator. Knowing the type of deficit is a key piece of information that is necessary for intervention planning. Analogue situations can be used to determine the type of deficit or to engage in testing of limits to see what the child is capable of under different conditions. Finally, structured or analogue observational assessments of behavior can be used to prompt low-frequency behavior that may otherwise be difficult to observe under naturalistic conditions in which a behavior may or may not occur.

The process of conducting observations under analogue conditions requires careful planning. The observers must know what behaviors they are specifically trying to prompt and create an analogue situation that is as close to the natural setting as possible. Even then, it is possible that the information gleaned from these types of observations will not provide data that is considered valid within the natural setting. Despite this challenge, analogue observations can be useful due to the amount of control the observer has over the situation and prompting specific behaviors (Merrell, 2003).

Benefits of Observational Assessments

Observational approaches to data collection have many associated benefits. As noted earlier, observations can provide direct information on how the child acts in either real-world or artificially constructed settings. In addition to evaluating student behavior, additional information can be collected about corresponding adult and peer behaviors as well as about the student's social environment. The ability to collect objective data on the child as well as the other participants in social situations can be particularly useful for evaluating social competency. Also, observational measures not only are useful in the initial data collection phase, but they can be used to evaluate skill development over time. Rating scales, in comparison, provide a static evaluation of the child's skills that is filtered through the perception of the rater. Using observational assessments allows practitioners to objectively evaluate the student's behavior in one or more different contexts. If done correctly, observational data can provide one of the most objective and valid pictures of a student's social functioning. Finally, once the observation procedure is refined, it can be used by teachers, parents, and students to collect data even in the absence of trained observers.

Limitations of Observational Assessments

Similar to other measurement tools, however, observations are not without drawbacks. Specific barriers to effective assessment when relying upon observational methods include poor preparation (e.g., inappropriate coding and recording systems) and thus poor implementation of the coding activities. The coding process is more complex and subjective than using rating scales; there is, therefore, greater potential for error in the measurement process. Conducting multiple observations across settings is labor and time intensive, if not impossible. As a result, it is not uncommon for an observer to never see the target behavior of concern. For reasons of pure timing, it is possible that the behavior observed may not be representative of the student's true social repertoire. Complicating the scheduling and planning of such observations is the fact that the number of observations required is often initially ambiguous (Merrell & Gimpel, 1998).

Further, observer-based limitations include issues of observer bias, reliability, observer drift, and student reactivity. Although these can be ameliorated with proper training and investment in the assessment process, teachers must still be conscious of the potential pitfalls in order to use the assessment technique effectively. Several suggestions for dealing with these pitfalls, besides training observers thoroughly, include calculating interobserver agreement and discussing differences in ratings; retraining observers after several observations to deal with observer drift; and having clear operational definitions of the behavior. For a further discussion of how practitioners can overcome barriers, see Merrell (1999). A final problem with observations is that because observing is the process of watching people interact, it can appear that attention is maintaining a behavior when, in fact, other functions or forces may be driving behavior.

INTERVIEWS

An interview is a purposeful form of communication that allows the interviewer to gather information by evaluating both the verbal and nonverbal responses of the interviewee. While an interview may seem like a conversation, it is a structured or at least semistructured communication that (1) is focused on topics relevant to understanding the student's social functioning, (2) is controlled primarily by the interviewer (although a good interviewer will be adept at balancing the need to get his or her questions answered with the interviewee's need to share information that he or she views as meaningful or relevant), and (3) progresses toward deeper understanding (Martin, 1988).

Interviews can be used to complement the information gathered using observations and rating scales. Because interviews involve extended communication, they allow practitioners to probe more deeply about particular skills. The combination of questions, follow-up questions, and interviewee insights can lead to a clearer and more thorough understanding of both internal and external factors that impact a particular skill or deficit. Interviews can be used to develop and refine our operational definitions of behavior as well as to gain insight into what the student is experiencing during the interactions we observe. We can also use interviews as an opportunity to follow up on responses from rating scales to better understand the thoughts, reasons, and experiences behind the ratings. Finally, interviews provide an opportunity to talk with each interviewee to identify which issues are most important to them, allowing practitioners to better prioritize what initial behaviors should be targeted for intervention.

Interviews with adults who spend time with the target student (e.g., teachers, parents, guardians), peers, and the student themselves are a widely used tool to help determine social skills strengths and deficits. As with rating scales, when conducting interviews, it is helpful to get the perspective of key stakeholders in the student's social environment. When collecting multiple perspectives, these perspectives will often differ, because each interviewee will have different experiences with the student and will even have different interpretations of the same experience. When responses differ, practitioners can use these differences to better understand how each response compares with what the practitioner sees as the true state of events and where the difference might be coming from. For example, when one teacher reports a skill deficit and a second teacher reports that the deficit does not exist, it could be that (1) the student uses the skill in one setting but not the other; (2) one teacher thinks the skill is important, whereas the other does not, and thus pays closer attention to the student's use of it; (3) one teacher may have a general negative perception of the student and endorses most skills as deficits rather than truly evaluating the presence or absence of each individual skill; or (4) one teacher may have several other students in his or her classroom whose behavior is much worse, and by comparison the target student is not seen as having a significant deficit. Understanding differences can contribute to intervention planning. In situation 1, the intervention would need to focus more on generalizing the skill, whereas for situation 3 the intervention may need to target increasing positive interactions between the teacher and the student in addition to any specific skill development.

Some general components of effective interviews are a person-centered approach (i.e., focused on trying to understand the interviewee's perspective); the use of active listening skills to build rapport and elicit accurate information; and having the right balance between structure and flexibility. Additionally, the interviewer must carefully consider what questions to ask, how the questions are structured (e.g., questions that are open ended, focused but not leading, direct, and phrased in a nonthreatening manner), and communicating to the interviewee at least some general guidelines on how to respond to interview questions. Finally, the interviewer should remind the interviewee how his or her responses will be used and what, if any, limits there will be to confidentiality for any information provided.

In deciding to use interviews as a social skills assessment tool, it is important to make sure to clearly identify what the interviewer wants to learn about the student's functioning through the interview process. To do this, the practitioner should begin by listing the skill domains that are relevant to the target student and then design questions to investigate specific aspects of the student's social functioning relative to each domain. Interviews, even more so than rating scales, can allow the practitioner to gain insight into the cognitions (thoughts, perceptions, attributions) and feelings that occur during social interactions. See Figure 6.3 for a list of suggested topics to assess as various internal and external aspects of a student's social skills and deficits. In order to do this, interviewers need to determine not only, for example, the current frequency and duration of the behavior but also its importance to those being interviewed and the extent to which changes in this behavior will lead to improvement for the student.

The following are some examples of general and social skills specific interview protocols:

- Examples of standard interview protocols include the Structured Developmental History associated with the BASC-2 (Reynolds & Kamphaus, 2004) and the Functional Assessment Interview (O'Neill et al., 1997). While these protocols are general, covering many different areas of development and functioning rather than focused specifically on social skills, many of the domains are relevant to students' social functioning and in some cases contain questions that can be adapted to ask about social functioning.
- Examples of interview approaches that are social skills specific include the Enactive Social Knowledge Interview (Mize & Ladd, 1988), the Home Interview with Child (Valente, 1994), and the Interpersonal Negotiation Strategies Interview (Schultz, Yeates, & Selman, 1989).

Benefits of Using Interviews

There are several benefits to using interviews, among them adaptability, a characteristic shared with observations. For example, the interviewing technique can be employed in highly structured formats with specific scripts and protocols, but it can also be free flowing and without structure, so that the interviewee may dictate the direction and pace of the interview (Merrell, 2001). Adaptability allows for decisions to be made based on what the assessment team believes to be best practice given the changing situations and contexts of the student in question. The interviewer has the option to change the protocol when necessary or remain static when the protocol is working.

Another positive and desirable attribute of interviews as a method of assessment is that they can provide interviewee insights regarding the environments in which problem behaviors occur and where specific intervention is warranted (Merrell, 2001). By interviewing parents, for example, the assessment team may be able learn additional information about context-specific antecedents of problem behaviors. Knowledge about school and home contexts and the student behaviors within those contexts provides the assessment team with more specific information that helps inform the direction of the behavior plan. Also, interviews with students themselves may provide feedback relative to the contexts in which that student has the most intense difficulty as well as insight into the intended function of problem behavior. Observation can tell us many important things about social skills or social deficits and the role of context, but validation

Any Informant

While these might seem like questions for just one informant, it is important to get the perspectives of all informants, because differences in opinion can provide a great deal of insight into social problems.

- What do they see as problems or specific behaviors of concern?
- Describe the frequency, duration, and intensity of target behaviors.
- When and where do the behaviors occur?
- What are the antecedents and consequences that happen before and after target behaviors? (Include both problem behaviors and appropriate behaviors.)
- What are possible replacement behaviors that could help the student get his or her needs met in a more appropriate way? What new skills would be meaningful for the target student or the significant adults in the student's life?
- Does the student have at least one friend? Generally, what is the student's status in the classroom?
- Identify the type of deficit: acquisition deficit, performance deficit, fluency deficit.
- Evaluate if there are any competing motivators or interfering responses that prevent the student from either learning or performing the skill.
- Include questions to evaluate for signs of depression, anxiety, and aggression/hostility.
- Ask about the student's strengths and interests, for example: What does he or she do well? What does he or she enjoy? What are conditions under which the student is successful?
- What things seem to motivate the student? Make sure to ask about potential internal motivators as well as external motivators.
- Begin with general questions and move to the specific.

Student Interviews

- Ask about self-perception generally as well as specifically in the areas of academic competence, achievement motivation, social competence, and peer acceptance.
- Use a pictures or scenarios as an analogue event to evaluate specific skills and the student's understanding of different situations. This approach is useful because practitioners can evaluate the student's actions or responses as well as his or her thoughts, perceptions, and emotions related to the situation by attending to follow-up considerations: for example, "What was the student thinking?" "Why did the student respond in a particular way?"
- Using an analogue situation or role play during an interview can also be helpful in evaluating the student's strategy use (or lack thereof) in various social situations. Very often students with disabilities have problems not because they do not have any strategies, but because they only have one strategy that they use in all situations, regardless of whether it is appropriate for that situation or not.
- Is there anything that is interfering with the student's ability to learn or perform different skills or behaviors?
- What could other people do to help them improve their social skills?
- What about school or social interactions do they enjoy?

Parent and Teacher Interviews

- What interventions have been tried in the past? What about those interventions were successful and what did not seem to help?
- Do both positive and problem behaviors happen in multiple settings?

(continued)

FIGURE 6.3. Topic considerations for social skills interviews.

- How are home and school perceptions similar and different?
- Of the student's skill deficits, which ones does the interviewee see as being absolutely necessary for success and which are considered to be unimportant or less important?
- If they could improve just one or two things for the student, what would they choose to target? This question is trying to get at social validity or what they think would be most meaningful for them as well as for the student.

Peer Interviews

- When interviewing peers, a practitioner can gather information about what those students think of as appropriate or inappropriate behavior, why they evaluate students in their class positively or negatively, or what strategies they use in social situations (Bierman, Smoot, & Aumiller, 1993).

FIGURE 6.3. *(continued)*

and new information from interviewing students and their stakeholders are invaluable. Additionally, interviews have been identified as an effective method for gathering data about behavior antecedents, consequences of problem social behaviors, intended functions of those behaviors, and the role of context in the development of students' social skills (Kratochwill & Bergan, 1990).

Interviews are person centered and can be used to establish rapport with a student, parent, or teacher. Interviews are a social interaction that can help the interviewer establish the foundation of a trusting relationship in a way that is not possible when using observations or rating scales. This rapport can be useful in helping the interviewee feel comfortable sharing private information and being willing to talk about weaknesses or failures. Interviewers can also use the interview to communicate empathy and an understanding of the unique issues that the student is facing. Through the use of open-ended questions, interviewers can invite the interviewee to contribute the different perspectives he or she may have on the topic. Because informants have more input into interview topics and direction, they can provide information that practitioners may not have otherwise thought to ask about. Parents, teachers, and students have the opportunity to bring up topics that are important to them during the interview process.

Finally, interviews allow for a direct evaluation of students' skills. During an interview, practitioners can directly observe a student's social skills. During the interview conversation, they can evaluate various aspects of social skills, such as nonverbal communication (e.g., eye contact, body language), language skills (vocabulary, expressive, and receptive language), pragmatics, and initiation skills. Furthermore, interviewing strategies can be expanded to use activities like role play (e.g., student and interviewer act out various social roles and situations and the student shares perceptions of what is and is not appropriate in specific contexts). Role-playing can be effective in demonstrating the value of specified social behaviors as perceived by the student and as an analogue setting to evaluate performance relative to societal expectations (Merrell, 2001; Steedly, Schwartz, Levin, & Luke, 2008).

Limitations of Using Interviews

Although there are benefits to using interviews to collect information about a student's social skills, many of those benefits have associated limitations. First, although the adaptability of interviews are an attractive feature, for interviews to be reliable and valid assessments of behavior, they must have some structure and be conducted by experienced professionals. Conducting a high-quality interview that is a reliable and valid assessment of a student's social skills requires the interviewer to have had intensive training, opportunities to practice interviewing, and feedback on performance. Even with such training, as compared with that for rating scales and observations, the evidence supporting the reliability and validity of interviews is lacking (Warren et al., 1999). This is even more true in the area of social skills evaluation, where there is not sufficient research evaluating the reliability and validity of these interviews, especially their use in real-world settings (Elliott & Gresham, 1987). The lack of specific evidence, however, does not mean that interviews should not be used, just that they should be used with caution.

High-quality training can reduce issues related to subjectivity. Which questions are asked, how those questions are asked, and evaluating what the responses to those questions mean are all open to individual preference and interpretation. They are subject to the skill of the interviewer. For interviews to be a source of useful data, the interviewer needs to be aware of his or her own biases and make sure that those biases do not inadvertently influence either client responses or which information is recorded. The following are factors that could affect the reliability and validity of the interview process:

- Questioning strategies. Interviewers who are unskilled in effective questioning strategies may accidently lead the interviewee to a particular answer. Children, in particular, are susceptible to leading questions or ineffective questioning approaches (Bjorklund, Bjorklund, Brown, & Cassel, 1998).
- Interviewer reaction to responses. If an interviewer has a strong reaction to a particular piece of information the student offers, it could either positively encourage the student to talk further about that topic or, negatively, make the student uncomfortable and thus hesitant to provide any additional information (Phillips & Gross, 2010).
- Impact of the interviewer's memory and attention to detail. Interviewers must make sure to capture all of the data and not rely solely on what he or she remembers. Otherwise, relevant information may be missed.
- Accurate evaluation of the information revealed and independent confirmation of interviewee responses. Children with social deficits may not always be the most accurate evaluators of their problems, or they may have difficulty accurately communicating what they know. Therefore, interviewers must take steps to seek independent confirmation of interviewee responses.

One final limitation of using interviews is that, even with trained interviewers and a prepared set of relevant questions, it is possible that the interviewer will fail to ask questions about behaviors that are important for each individual student. When developing an interview protocol, it is difficult to identify every possible relevant topic. This problem can be addressed by waiting to finalize the interview protocol until initial data have been collected about the student. This will allow the interview questions to be adapted to match topics that are relevant for that student. Additionally, interviewers can allow for higher flexibility (be more willing to deviate from the prearranged script) during the interview to increase the likelihood that relevant information will be captured. Practitioners, however, must acknowledge that being flexible and making changes to the questions could result in changes to the reliability and validity of the interview results. In some cases, the changes may be positive, but there is no way the interviewer can be sure without conducting a reliability and validity analysis of each protocol for each student.

FUNCTIONAL BEHAVIORAL ASSESSMENT

Functional behavioral assessment (FBA) is a method of evaluating a possible purpose or "function" that a behavior is serving for the student. The methods used in a functional analysis were developed by Iwata, Dorsey, Slifer, Bauman, and Richman (1982/1994). There are four major functions that a behavior can serve (identified by Iwata et al., 1982/1994): (1) positive social (attention), (2) positive automatic (self-stimulation or alleviation of boredom), (3) negative social (escape from unpleasant or unwanted situation), and (4) negative automatic (alleviate pain). Other functions have been suggested, including access to a tangible item and control. In evaluating problem behaviors, the two most likely functions of behavior are escape/avoidance and attention.

In order to develop an initial hypothesis as to the function of the behavior, professionals must evaluate the setting events, antecedents or triggers, and consequences that are affecting the behavior. Setting events can include (1) physiological factors (e.g., illness, pain, hunger, medication side effects); (2) psychological factors (e.g., the presence of a major depressive episode or cognitive impairments); (3) environmental factors (e.g., classroom desk arrangements, noise level, peer disruption or isolation; unsafe conditions); and (4) instructional factors (e.g., low, changing, or unclear expectations, overly easy or difficult classroom assignments).

Setting events are different from antecedents. Setting events are global and generally make a behavior more or less likely to occur. Antecedents are specific and directly precede or trigger the onset of a behavior. Consequences are anything that happens after (intentionally or unintentionally) a problem behavior that makes the behavior either more or less likely to occur. Multiple assessment tools (e.g., observations, behavior rating scales, and interviews) can be used during the FBA process to collect information about setting events, antecedents, and maintaining consequences of behavior. These assessment tools, however, can only provide practitioners with a hypothesis as to the function of the behavior. The only way to know for sure that the correct function has been identified is to conduct a functional analysis. In a functional analysis, the practitioner repeatedly exposes the students to four conditions—attention, escape, alone, and control—to determine which results in an increase in the behavior. For a more thorough explanation of functional analysis, see Iwata et al. (1982/1994).

Benefits of FBA

An FBA is considered the most comprehensive and thorough assessment method to use with individual students who exhibit behaviors that interfere with their social success in the classroom. It is a process that evaluates all factors that could possibly impact the performance of the behavior (antecedents, consequences, setting events, environmental factors), and then all of these data are used to develop a hypothesis about the function of the behavior, which can be empirically tested. It is also the assessment process that is most directly connected to intervention planning, because it provides standard empirical data that can be used to identify a specific function, antecedent, or maintaining consequence. Having specific evidence about a particular behavior takes the guesswork out of choosing intervention components such as replacement behaviors or altering maintaining consequences. It makes the whole intervention development process more effective and efficient.

Limitations of FBA

Even though FBAs can provide much rich data in the assessment of social skills, they also have drawbacks. The experimental analysis of behavior involves a complex process that can be impractical in a school setting. For example, conducting 30 repetitions of the four standard conditions plus any nonstandard conditions that are necessary to understand the behavior of an individual student is incredibly time intensive and requires the expertise of someone who has training in behavior analysis. This criticism has been addressed by developing a brief approach to conducting a functional assessment (Vollmer & Northup, 1996). In these brief approaches, researchers have demonstrated that sessions that are shorter and fewer in number can be used by typical school personnel in a manner that is nearly as reliable and valid as the standard, complete functional analysis. Another criticism is that an FBA is less appropriate for skill deficits, since it is not possible to determine the function of a nonbehavior. In these cases, it is appropriate to use the FBA process to develop hypotheses about the type of skill deficit (i.e., lack of skills, motivation, experience, or support), so that the intervention can be accurately matched to the student's level of need (Daly, Witt, Martens, & Dool, 1997).

Practitioners wanting more information on conducting FBAs should see the following resources:

Cipani, E., & Schock, K. M. (2011). *Functional behavioral assessment, diagnosis, and treatment* (2nd ed.). New York: Springer.

O'Neill, R. E., Horner, R. H., Albin, R. W., Sprague, J. R., Storey, K., & Newton, J. S. (1997). *Functional assessment and program development for problem behavior: A practical handbook* (2nd ed.). Pacific Grove, CA: Brooks/Cole.

Steege, M. W, Watson, T. S., & Gresham, F. M. (2009). *Conducting school-based functional assessment: A practitioner's guide* (2nd ed.). New York: Guilford Press.

SOCIOMETRIC RATINGS

Sociometric ratings (peer rating, ranking, and nomination of target students) can be used to measure constructs such as peer acceptance that are related to social skills (Merrell, 2001). Sociometric techniques, however, have several weaknesses when it comes to individual intervention planning. They are time and procedurally intensive (one must obtain assessment consent from the parents of every student in the classroom and potentially multiple classrooms). Additionally, the evidence to support their usefulness in intervention planning has not been well documented. Because of these weaknesses, we have chosen to omit a description of how to conduct sociometric ratings from this chapter. For an in-depth discussion of sociometric and other analogue techniques for assessing aspects of social behavior, see Hintze, Stoner, and Bull (2000).

WHAT TO MEASURE

The previous sections give an overview of the different methods practitioners can use to measure aspects of social competency. These methods, however, have been aimed at answering questions about specific assessment methods. In this final assessment topic, we identify the broad questions practitioners should seek to answer during their assessment.

- What are the student's social strengths and weaknesses? In order for intervention planning to be successful, we have to measure not only a student's deficits but also the skills that exist in his or her repertoire.
- What are features of the environment that could be altered to support the development of social competence, antecedents that make the use of social skills more or less likely, and consequences that may be maintaining problem behaviors?
- What is the function of the problem behavior? Interventions for problems that are maintained by attention will look different than problems maintained by escape.
- Are problems due to a skill deficit? The answer to this question will affect where an intervention begins. If it is a skills deficit, then an intervention must first target skill instruction.
- Are problems due to a performance deficit? (That is, a student knows what to do but does not consistently demonstrate the skill.) In the case of a performance deficit, the intervention can begin by promoting student use of the skill. Performance deficits can be due to (1) lack of motivation, (2) competing reinforcers, (3) internal factors (lack of confidence or high levels of anxiety), or (4) lack of practice or adequate feedback.
- What is the current level of behavior? A final purpose of assessment is to document a baseline. It is impossible to determine appropriate interventions or to evaluate whether skills are improving without knowing the student's current levels of social functioning.

PROGRESS MONITORING AND EVALUATING PROGRESS

Data-based decision making depends on two key features: (1) having good data on which a decision can be based and (2) actually reviewing and using the data when making a decision. Although both of these components are on some level self-evident, unfortunately in practice they are all too often overlooked. For one reason or another, data are not collected or we have wonderful data that has been dutifully recorded and filed but never reviewed. Figure 6.4 is an example of a simple chart for collecting progress-monitoring data on a behavior such as the number of times a child engages in social initiation. This kind of record not only collects the data but also allows for easy graphing of the data to help evaluate progress.

Monitoring and evaluating progress involves practitioners looking both backward and forward. We look backward to evaluate the integrity and effectiveness of the intervention. If we did not meet our goals in either of those two areas, then we must revise our plan. We also use the ongoing data to identify next steps needed to support continuing development of the student's skills until all of the student's goals have been achieved.

The following are resources for designing measures to evaluate student progress and intervention effectiveness.

> Lavelle, L. (1998). *Practical charts for managing behavior.* Austin, TX: Pro-Ed.—This book contains over 100 pages of user-friendly charts and graphs that can be used to monitor student behavior. This is an excellent resource for teachers or other school practitioners looking for many different examples of how skills change can be measured.
> Riley-Tillman, T. C., & Burns, M. K. (2009). *Single-case design for measuring response to intervention.* New York: Guilford Press.—While this book is not specific to social skills, it is a user-friendly resource for helping practitioners use a single-case design approach to evaluate intervention effectiveness. The book includes easy-to-use reproducible graphs and forms.

Goal Attainment Scale

One additional tool that is useful for evaluating behavior change is the goal attainment scale (GAS). These scales are an effective, free, and user-friendly mechanism for monitoring progress and evaluating intervention effectiveness. Researchers and practitioners alike have found the GAS to be useful in evaluating behaviors in a wide variety of settings (e.g., schools, home, health care, sports medicine). The basic components the GAS are (1) a long-term goal, (2) three to five behavior benchmarks, (3) identification of who will be responsible for monitoring and reviewing progress, (4) an expected completion date (a statement of how long it should take to achieve this long-term goal), and (5) a schedule for reviewing and evaluating progress. See Figure 6.5 for a sample GAS progress monitoring form.

Using the GAS structure, a combination of short-term benchmarks and long-term goals allows practitioners to evaluate skill development in a way that continually increases expectations as skills improve. The three to five behavioral benchmarks are

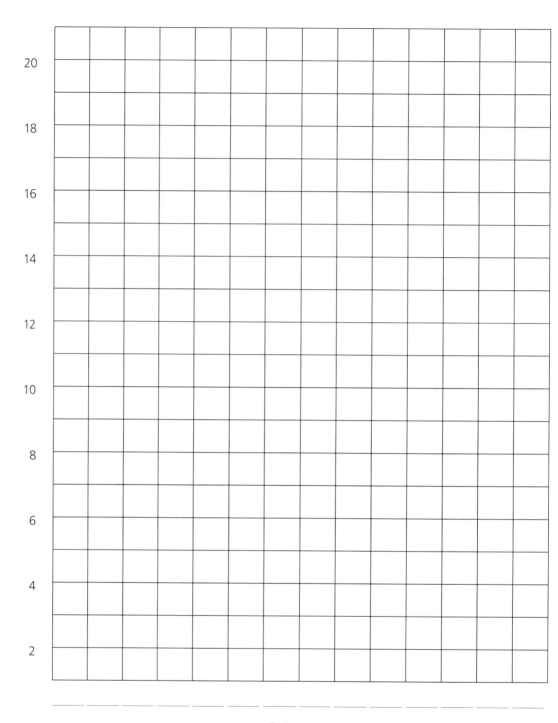

Date

FIGURE 6.4. Progress monitoring chart for social initiations.

Figure courtesy of Jennifer L. Schroeder. From *Promoting Social Skills in the Inclusive Classroom* by Kimber L. Wilkerson, Aaron B. T. Perzigian, and Jill K. Schurr. Copyright 2014 by The Guilford Press. Permission to photocopy this figure is granted to purchasers of the book for personal use only (see copyright page for details). Purchasers may download a larger version of this figure from *www.guilford.com/p/wilkerson*.

Goal: _____

Estimated start and end dates? _____

How often will progress toward the goal be reviewed? _____
_____

Who will rate the behavior? _____
_____

How often will the behavior be rated? _____
_____

Benchmarks:

+2 _____

+1 _____

 0 _____

−1 _____

−2 _____

Behavior Graph

	1	2	3	4	5	6	7	8	9	10	11	12	13	14	15
+2															
+1															
0															
−1															
−2															

Time Frame (check one): _____ Class Period _____ Day _____ Week

_____ Other: _____

FIGURE 6.5. Goal attainment scale progress monitoring form.

used to evaluate day-to-day progress of the behavior. These benchmarks are commonly structured as follows:

+2: What the behavior would look like if it *improved*? When identifying what behaviors would be considered improvement, make sure to use small, gradual increments. Setting the bar too high to reach a +2 rating will be discouraging to both teachers and students.

0: What is the current level of behavior or a description of what the behavior looks like on an *average* day? (Baseline data can be used to develop the 0-level description of behavior.)

–2: What would the behavior look like on a *bad* day? Here you can describe what the behavior looks like when there is a spike in problem behaviors.

The in-between ratings of +1 and –1 can be used for when the behavior is somewhere in between the 0 rating and either +2 or –2. The descriptions of each benchmark should be observable and measurable. Practitioners can use the same process for developing behavioral benchmarks that they used to define behaviors for observations (see pp. 103–104 for more information on this process). What makes this scale so easy to use is that once the student is receiving consistent ratings of +2, a new set of benchmarks can be created by simply sliding the benchmarks down the scale (the +2 rating becomes the –2, and a new +2 rating is developed). The responsiveness of the GAS (having benchmarks that can be moved up or down to increase or decrease difficulty) makes it easier to keep students at an instructional level (70–85% success rate). The long-term goal can then be identified as having been achieved when the +2 rating matches the long-term goal. This makes the process of monitoring student progress and identifying when the intervention goal has been completed objective and clear. Once the long-term goals of an intervention have been achieved, support for the student can transition into generalization and maintenance phases.

An additional benefit of the GAS is its simplicity. The -2 to +2 ratings with clearly defined behaviors mean that it can be easily used by busy classroom teachers (all they have to do is write down a number for each rating period), shared across staff for consistency in rating behavior, and modified for students to use as a self-monitoring tool. Not only is it easy to use, but the results are easy to interpret and share. Analyzing the data points can be graphed out. The pattern of data points across time and settings can be helpful in identifying areas where the intervention is working well and where improvement is needed. For more information on how to develop and use goal attainment scales, see the following:

Kiresuk, T. J., Smith, A., & Cardillo, J. E. (Eds.). (1994). *Goal attainment scaling: Theory and measurement*. Florence, KY: Psychology Press (Taylor & Francis).

Single-Case Design

Use a single-case design approach to test out your intervention. For many professionals working in the realities of a school, using a single-case design can sound like a pie-in-the-sky ideal of a university researcher. However, we believe that using this method to test out an intervention is an effective and efficient use of professional time. The days spent testing out an intervention will (1) help the professional determine whether the right intervention for a particular student has been chosen, and whether the intervention results in a sufficient level of behavior change to justify the investment of time and resources; (2) serve as a debugging opportunity—one can conduct a dry run and work out implementation problems; and (3) provide effectiveness data, which can be useful in convincing people who are showing signs of resistance that the intervention is worth a try. For a complete overview of practical applications of single-case designs in the schools, see the following references:

Riley-Tillman, T. C., & Burns, M. K. (2009). *Evaluating educational interventions: Single-case design for measuring response to intervention*. New York: Guilford Press.
Skinner, C. H. (2005). *Single-subject designs for school psychologists*. New York: Routledge.

ENSURING AND EVALUATING INTERVENTION INTEGRITY AND ACCEPTABILITY

Witt and Elliott (1985) have proposed a four-part structure for evaluating intervention success: treatment integrity, treatment acceptability, treatment use, and treatment effectiveness. In this section, we review how treatment acceptability and integrity can affect the effectiveness and use of individual interventions. Acceptability of an intervention is a major component of intervention integrity. People have to believe that the intervention will be effective at changing behavior (Lennox & Miltenberger, 1990). Kazdin (1980) defined acceptability as the professional judgments made in evaluating an invention in terms fairness, intrusiveness, and reasonableness. In a collaborative situation where the professional judgment of everyone involved is respected, questions related to acceptability must be addressed. The responsibility for addressing these questions regarding intervention acceptability must lie with all team members. Cowan and Sheridan (2003) reinvestigated factors that influence teacher rating of acceptability in real-world settings. They found that factors related to the complexity and the severity of the intervention were positively related to acceptability ratings. The following are suggestions for evaluating and increasing intervention acceptability:

- Positive interventions are consistently rated as being more acceptable by both teachers and parents (Elliott, 1988).

- More complex and intensive interventions are found to be more acceptable when a child's problems are severe (Cowan & Sheridan, 2003; Elliott, 1988).

- Is the intervention feasible? Just because an intervention has high-quality evidence supporting its effectiveness does not mean it is always the best choice. If staff do not perceive the school as having the resources or professional skill to carry out the intervention, they are unlikely to rate it as acceptable. Schools should consider the cost effectiveness and the competence of their staff when choosing an intervention (Lennox & Miltenberger, 1990).

- Teams need to create an environment where teachers feel safe raising concerns about the acceptability of a treatment, being aware of pressure to conform. Conformity pressure can be reduced by discussing intervention plan ideas with key team members (teachers, parents, students) before any group meetings. Premeeting sessions provide opportunities to express concerns about the intervention in a one-on-one setting.

- Lack of acceptability sometimes comes from lack of understanding. Talking about intervention options with key stakeholders in advance of any decision meeting can provide more time to answer questions or disseminate additional information about the intervention, why it was chosen for this student, and evidence of effectiveness.

- Teachers need to take responsibility for speaking up if they find an intervention or intervention component unacceptable. Those who are reluctant to say something in front of the whole group should find someone they trust and express their concerns before the intervention begins. It is not acceptable to agree to an intervention publicly and then implement it half-heartedly or not at all because it is not well liked. This approach will only result in more negative experiences for the student who is the focus of the intervention and possibly make the behavior more difficult to change.

- Student perceptions of acceptability should also be considered. Someone on the intervention planning team should talk to the student to see if he or she finds the intervention acceptable; this is part of person-centered planning. Additionally, having student buy-in increases the likelihood an intervention will be successful. What is said in this acceptability conversation will depend on the student's age, developmental level, and readiness for change. For some students, it is appropriate to ask if they are willing to participate in the intervention (although when asking a yes–no question, the professional must be prepared not to implement if the response is "no"). If the plan is to implement the intervention regardless of what the student says, then only ask for feedback on the parts of the intervention that can be altered or on what motivators would increase the student's willingness to participate.

- Finally, everyone needs to be flexible and be willing to give interventions with sufficient supporting evidence a real chance to work.

Ensuring intervention integrity at tier 3 involves the same types of activities as ensuring intervention integrity at tiers 1 and 2. Researchers who have studied how different levels of intervention integrity affect the effectiveness individual interventions have found that high-integrity interventions result in students acquiring more skills in a shorter span of time (Wilder, Atwell, & Wine, 2006). Intervention integrity and intervention effectiveness must be measured at the same time if true effectiveness of the intervention is to be accurately evaluated. Without information on integrity, we cannot know if an intervention failed because it was not the right intervention or because it was not being implemented completely or correctly. Additionally, integrity data can help consultants know which parts of the intervention may require additional support or training.

School professionals can take the following steps to increase and evaluate the integrity of an intervention:

confident in one's own abilities. Good reinforcement systems seek to build these long-term reinforcers into intervention plans.

- When using reinforcers, remember to have a menu of different choices. If you use the same reinforcer all the time, the student will eventually become satiated and the reinforcer will no longer be motivation.
- Carefully consider the schedule of reinforcement (how often reinforcement will be given). Reinforcement delivery should be greatly increased any time students do something new or difficult. As students increase their skills, external rewards should be faded out.
- A variety of differential reinforcement procedures (i.e., reinforcing walking to eliminate running) can be used to increase the effectiveness of this approach to intervention.
- Use shaping, a process where the student is reinforced for performing gradually closer approximations of the appropriate behavior.
- Anything that does not result in an increase in the target behavior is not a reinforcer.

As with other interventions in this section, this is only a brief overview of factors that promote the effective application of reinforcement techniques.

PUNISHMENT

Punishment is anything that happens after a behavior that makes the behavior less likely to occur. This definition is important to remember. All too often we do things that we call punishment but that never result in the reduction of targeted problem behaviors. In fact, sometimes problem behaviors increase. This is especially true when the function of the behavior is not used when identifying punishers. For example, a child is sent to the principal's office when he or she acts out in class. If the function of the child's disruptive behavior is to escape, then sending the child out of the classroom actually reinforces the behavior rather than punishing it. Punishers should only be used for targeted purposes when the function of the behavior has been clearly identified. Additionally, punishers should only continue to be used over time when they result in an immediate reduction in negative behaviors. If problem behaviors remain stable over time, then whatever we are doing is either not effective or not efficient at reducing the problem behavior and, therefore, actually not a punisher.

While punishment can be effective at changing behaviors, it also comes with greater risks than antecedent or reinforcement procedures. Two significant risks involve damaging relationships and keeping attention focused on the things the students are doing wrong. Because punishment involves delivering a negative, over time the students may begin to associate negative emotions with the person who delivers the punishment. High use of punishment can damage the teacher–student relationship, which is necessary for successful behavior change. For students at the individual level, one of the most important impacts of an effective intervention is to shift the focus from the things the students do wrong to the things they can do right. Punishment, unfortunately, keeps the focus on the students' deficits rather than their strengths.

Another reason to avoid the use of punishers with students who need individual intervention plans is that exposure to repeated punishers can reinforce their sense of failure and helplessness. When considering the inclusion of a punisher as part of an individual intervention plan, one question to ask is: "What could we as practitioners do that is really more punishing than the life they are currently living?" All too often the answer to that question is: very little. In order to reach an individual level of intervention, students have more than likely failed multiple times. Students with social deficits typically have poor relationships with both adults and peers. Punishers, therefore, should be one of the last options for students experiencing social difficulties.

TOKEN ECONOMIES

Token economies are when tangible items (e.g., tokens, tickets) are given to students when they engage in a target behavior or demonstrate a particular skill. Those tokens can then be exchanged for reinforcers. Tangible items should be used in token systems, not points. Especially for younger children, numbers are very abstract concepts. Therefore, earning 100 or 1,000 points is meaningless, but seeing tokens accumulate in the token jar is a physical manifestation of the things they have done right. They can concretely see what they have earned. Sometimes in token economies, a method called cost–response is used. This is where points or tokens that have been earned for good behavior are taken away when the students act inappropriately or fail to exhibit the correct behavior. This procedure is not recommended in schools. If the students' motivation/rewards system has been designed correctly, then the failure to earn a token is sufficiently punishing to change the behavior. Trying to take away tokens from students can result in a power struggle that keeps the focus on the inappropriate behavior, extends time off task for both the student and the teacher, and may escalate the severity of the problem behavior. There is no evidence to support any benefit of including cost–response in a school-based individual intervention plan.

EXTINCTION

Extinction occurs when (1) a behavior has been previously reinforced, (2) the delivery of the reinforcement is discontinued, and (3) the behavior stops because it is no longer being reinforced (Mittenberger, 2012). It is important to note that there is a common event known as an extinction burst that can occur between Steps 2 and 3 of the extinction process. An *extinction burst* is a temporary increase in the severity of the problem behavior designed to regain access to the previous reinforcer. This concept is particularly important for schools to understand, because extinction is a natural component of any intervention plan. In schools the extinction process typically follows a common path. First, problem behaviors are regularly reinforced (usually unintentionally) in typical responses to problem behavior (sending a child out of the classroom when he or she becomes disruptive often reinforces the disruptive behavior). Next, an individual intervention plan is implemented, and that reinforcement abruptly stops. Finally, in response to the removal of the reinforcement, the student's behavior initially

Example of an Extinction Burst: Aggression

Take, for example, the student whose aggressive behavior is maintained by escape. Whenever the student becomes aggressive in the classroom, he is sent to the principal's office. Then the team decides that going to the principal's office isn't working, so they design an intervention where the child will take his work and go to another class to complete it under the supervision of a teacher who has a free period. When the intervention is implemented, there is a spike in the child's aggressive behavior. Instead of just throwing things at people, the child begins to hit people and destroy property. The intervention is then discontinued and the child is suspended for aggressive behavior. If the aggression escalates, the intervention will likely be discontinued and the length of removal increased to out-of-school suspension.* By withdrawing the intervention and again allowing the child to escape, the aggressive behavior has not only been reinforced but has been reinforced at a higher level. So now instead of just throwing things, it is more likely that the child will hit people. It is this progression of reinforcement, withdrawal of reinforcement, extinction burst, and reinstatement of reinforcement that can cause low levels of aggressive behavior to escalate, with the student engaging in increasingly more serious acts of aggression toward other students, staff, and property and engaging in acts of self-harm (e.g., scratching, biting, cutting) or self-endangerment (e.g., running from the school building, going into unsafe areas of a school building). This same progression of acting-out behavior can be seen in the grocery store scenario: A child wants an item so she screams. The parent gives in and inadvertently reinforces the screaming. During the next trip to the grocery store, the parent decides to stand firm and say "no" despite the screaming. However, when the child starts to grab things off the shelf and throw them on the ground, the parent relents and the child is again reinforced. During the next outing, the child's outbursts are likely to be longer and more severe. While it is difficult not to give in when faced with an upset or aggressive child, adults must always be aware of the possibility of unintentionally reinforcing a problem behavior.

---

*A note about suspension: Suspension of children who are struggling in school or who do not like school is a powerful reinforcer for problem behaviors (Tobin & Sugai, 1996). When elementary school-age students are suspended, they cannot be left home alone. As is often the case, to accommodate the suspension, a parent must take time off from work, the children must stay with a family member, or they go to day care. They escape from somewhere they do not want to be and instead spend the day receiving attention from preferred adults. Even one suspension can result in exhibitions of intense, sustained aggression in order to try to get access again to the reinforcement of being sent home. Schools should develop an in-house alternative to out-of-school suspension where the child is not allowed to escape from school and does not received additional attention (sometimes in-school suspension can result in a child visiting with the suspension room teacher for much of the day, as it is difficult to punish a child for 7–8 hours straight) and a functional assessment of the behavior can be immediately started.

gets worse. When this increase in negative behavior appears, school staff may discontinue or modify the intervention because they see the increase in problem behavior as evidence that the intervention is not working. When we start and stop interventions in this manner, two problems occur: (1) The problem behavior can become more resistant to intervention (because the students learn that interventions stop when their behavior gets worse) and (2) the behavior is reinforced at a high level (the new, more severe problem behavior now may become the standard behavior). This extinction/extinction burst process is an all too common mechanism by which severe aggressive behaviors develop in schools. Finally, when implementing an intervention plan, practitioners should also be familiar with the principle of *spontaneous recovery*. Spontaneous recovery is when a previous problem behavior reappears out of nowhere. In this situation, there is no trigger. It is not an indicator of failure or the child moving backward. It is just a reappearance of a previous problem behavior. When this spontaneous recovery happens, teachers must make sure to moderate their reactions. It is usually just as disconcerting for the student as it is for the teacher. The best response to this type of random reoccurrence of a problem behavior is to down play the incident and provide the student with some temporary additional support.

Time-Out

Time-out is when a student is removed from a positive environment as a method of either punishing (reducing) or reinforcing (increasing) a particular behavior. For time-out to be effective, the environment the student is being removed from has to be positive. If it is not positive, the negative behavior will be rewarded by allowing the student to escape from a nonpreferred task. The following are two examples of time-out, demonstrating in the first scenario the right way to use it and in the second scenario the wrong way to use it. Scenario 1: A student really likes doing science experiments but has difficulty working with others in his or her lab group and exhibits bossy behavior or uses inappropriate language with them. He is given a time-out in order to reduce these problem behaviors. Scenario 2: The student hates science labs, doesn't like his lab mates, and exhibits inappropriate behavior with them. When he is removed from the group with a time-out, he learns that the inappropriate behavior is an easy way to get out of doing something he doesn't like, and the time-out only reinforces (increases) the problem behavior. Time-out should not be used for escape-motivated behavior.

Finally, there are differences among time-out, time to cool down, and needing a break. Sometimes when students are getting upset, they may need to move to a quieter or less crowded area to help themselves calm down. A cool-down strategy can be an effective prevention or intervention strategy for students who are having difficulty dealing with anger, frustration, or anxiety, but it is one that is quite different from time-out. Cool-down strategies usually involve (1) teaching of early warning signs of anger, anxiety, or frustration; (2) teaching and practicing using relaxation strategies to address these; and (3) giving students opportunities to practice and get feedback on using the cool-down process when they are calm and relaxed as well as when they are getting upset. Additionally, some students may have sensory issues or just get overwhelmed. For these students (especially at the beginning of an intervention when they are just learning coping skills), they may need the option to take occasional breaks. When using a break as an intervention strategy, (1) they should not be punitive in nature; (2) students should be taught when, why, and how to use their break opportunities; and (3) breaks should be faded out over time as skills develop.

Social Learning Approaches to Skills Development

Strategies that incorporate social learning components rely on utilizing the child's social environment as a mechanism of change (Bandura & Walters, 1963; Bandura, 1977). Social learning theories posit that social behaviors are learned through peer observation and reinforcement of those behaviors by others (Elliott & Busse, 1991). Thus, interventions that include components such as behavior modeling and role-playing techniques fall in this category. In settings where progress may be influenced by peer behaviors (such as cooperative groups), socially withdrawn students have opportunities to interact with peers and practice social competencies needed for peer socialization (Elliott & Busse, 1991). When developing intervention plans, teachers can begin by looking for social opportunities that already exist in their classroom. Then, these preexisting social situations can be used as opportunities for modeling, practice, and feedback related to targeted social skills.

Modeling

The components of modeling include (1) having a model (adult or peer) demonstrate the behavior, (2) provide the target student an opportunity to repeat the behavior, and (3) provide the model and the target student with feedback on their performance, including praise for the parts of the action completed successfully (it is important to focus on feedback related to what was done right versus actions that were not successfully completed). In order for modeling to be successful, the student must (1) be capable of engaging in the target skill (choose a behavior that already exists in the student's skill repertoire); (2) pay attention to the performance of the behavior (it is useful to cue the student to pay attention to the model); and (3) be motivated to repeat the behavior. Children are more likely to model behavior that is exhibited by either high-status peers or students they see as being like them. Thus, teachers should think carefully about which student they choose to be the model. For example, teachers often choose high-performing students to model a behavior. Children who are struggling may see the behavior as something only good students do rather than something that they themselves are capable of doing. Finally, keep the behaviors simple; behaviors that are too complex are unlikely to be attempted.

Role Playing

Role-playing intervention strategies take advantage of creative implementation opportunities (e.g., acting and storytelling) to teach and reinforce social skills. Children's books and scripts from curricula identified in Chapters 3 and 4 can be great sources of role-playing scenarios. Students can also be asked to make up their role play, which can increase the social validity of this intervention approach. Role playing can be used as part of academic instruction in classes such as reading, literature, or social studies. When interventions can be constructed so that they promote social development during academics, it benefits the students by promoting generalization of skills and it benefits the teacher because it takes less time away from learning.

Cognitive Approaches to Skills Development

Cognitive interventions focus on altering a student's thoughts, perceptions, or thought processes. For example, students may have the necessary prerequisite skills to appropriately initiate social interactions, but every time they approach a peer they may use negative self-statements to sabotage the interaction or may inappropriately interpret the other students as responding negatively when, in fact, the responses were positive. Cognitive interventions may also target cognitive skills (such as attention or memory). Sometimes students fail in social situations because they do not pay attention to the correct cues or they don't remember what steps to take once a social interaction has been initiated. Because cognitive strategies involve altering a student's internal thought, they play an important role in promoting generalization and maintenance of skills. Some effective cognitive interventions include developing problem-solving skills, improving self-efficacy, metacognitive strategies (teaching students about strategy use and strategy selection), cognitive restructuring (changing how students interpret events), reattribution of reasons for success or failure, developing coping skills, and use of social stories.

Scripts of Social Stories

Using a social story, children can learn about different types of social situations and what skills are appropriate for those situations. Social stories can be tailored so that they reflect the individual situations that a particular child is facing. For an overview on how to use social stories and interventions, see Reynhout and Carter (2006).

Cognitive-Behavioral Approaches to Skills Development

The combination of cognitive and behavioral approaches is one example of how theories can be combined in a way that builds on each other's strengths and mitigates some of their limitations. A combination of cognitive and behavioral theories can be used to develop interventions that target a student's internal regulation of social behavior (Elliott & Busse, 1991). Coaching, for example, is a widely utilized cognitive-behavioral intervention procedure. In a coaching intervention, a "coach," who can be a teacher, school psychologist, or in some situations even a peer, identifies and rehearses with the target student when to recognize and how to perform expected social behaviors. Cognitive-behavior interventions are also created when practitioners combine the behavioral and cognitive interventions described previously. For example, social or interpersonal problem-solving interventions can be used to teach skills, and antecedent and consequence strategies can be implemented to promote the use of those skills in a variety of settings. In a cognitive-behavioral social problem-solving intervention, social problems are initially divided into smaller, more easily identifiable steps. These include identifying and defining the problem, exploring alternate reactions to the problem, considering the consequences of each reaction, and choosing the most appropriate reaction (Elliott & Busse, 1991). Reinforcers may then be used to increase the student's use of the skills he or she just learned. While not directed specifically at social skills, practitioners interested in school-based applications of cognitive-behavioral intervention should see Mayer, Van Acker, Lochman, and Gresham (2011).

Teaching Strategies

Teaching strategies are a central component of any individual plan to improve social skills. We use direct skills instruction strategies to address acquisition deficits. For performance or fluency difficulties, students must be provided the opportunity to have frequent practice combined with useful feedback on what the student is doing as well as that with which he or she is struggling. Therefore, regardless of the root of the difficulty, it can be addressed by some form of teaching similar to the strategies used for academic subjects such as math or reading.

Coaching

As educators, many of us are familiar with common teaching metaphors: "Sage on the stage" and "Guide on the side." Coaching, as an instructional strategy, is in line with the latter; rather than instruct knowledge in a front-and-center outlet, coaching revolves around guiding and assisting the student with ways to facilitate self-instigated learning. Thus, coaching a student with social skills development involves identifying specific areas upon which to focus and then guiding the acquisition of skills by role playing, practicing, and evaluating consequences of social choices. In many instances, students with disabilities are not afforded opportunities to take direction of their own learning. A coaching method employed at the tertiary level allows students with social difficulties to practice self-determination and become agents in their own social development. Thus, a coach's role is to provide advice, suggestions, and support while students direct their own social skills acquisition. Research indicates that self-directed learning, in many content areas, facilitated by a teacher's coaching role, increases students' engagement with the material and improves their classroom performance (see Ness & Middleton, 2012, for a presentation of one such model).

Task Analysis and Chaining

When teaching a skill, a *task analysis* can be used to break down the skill into discrete steps or parts. For example, if a student is struggling with ways to engage in appropriate, two-direction conversations (e.g., being able to read turn-taking cues), a teacher can break up conversation engagement into multiple small steps, which combine to form conversation. In this example, conversation is the task that has been analyzed, or broken down, into smaller steps. A two-way conversation typically includes an exchange of common niceties, questions and answers, and appropriate responses to the other. If the overall goal is for the student to learn how to engage in conversation, each of those independent steps can be broken down and mastered individually as discrete skills and then combined to form a conversation.

As part of a task analysis, practitioners should evaluate cognitive as well as physical components that are necessary for a task to be successfully completed. Once the parts of a task or skill have been identified, it is much easier to decide how to teach the skill. Some parts the student may know how to do and only need to be reinforced, and other parts may be novel and require direct skills instruction. In addition to helping target acquisition versus performance deficit aspects, a task analysis can be used to teach a behavior through *chaining*. There are three types of chaining-related procedures: forward chaining, backward chaining, and total task presentation. Using forward chaining, the student is taught the first step identified in the task analysis. Once the student can perform that first step fluently, subsequent steps are added until the student can do the complete task. Forward chaining is most often used for skills that are not currently in the student's repertoire. In backward chaining, the student begins by performing the last step identified in the task analysis and moves backward to the first step. Total task presentation is when the student is expected to perform all of the steps at once, often with the support of prompts, cues, or reminders that are faded over time. Backward chaining and total task presentation are best for skills where there is either a performance or fluency type of deficit.

Behavior Skills Training

Behavior skills training (BST) is an evidence-based process for helping students acquire skills. It includes several intervention components that have been described earlier in the chapter. BST include four steps: modeling, delivering specific instructions about behavior expectations, rehearsal time to practice the behavior after seeing it and receiving instruction, and providing feedback on their performance that focuses on what was done correctly. BST may require that practitioners conduct a task analysis in order to break down a behavior or social skills into teachable parts. Two specific types of BST procedures are shaping and chaining. Shaping is defined as "differential reinforcement of successive approximations of the target behavior until the person exhibits the target behavior" (Mittenberger, 2012, p. 160). Chaining occurs when a skill is broken down into a set of sequential steps. The steps are taught and reinforced, with initial reinforcements provided for completing a single step and subsequent reinforcements provided for completing an increasingly greater number of steps until the whole behavior can be completed.

Positive Teacher–Student Relationships

Establishing positive relationships with students is a central feature of any attempt to change their behavior. While this is a common strategy for promoting positive behavior, it is particularly important for students with social difficulties. Positive relationships facilitate interventions such as modeling, practice, feedback, and reinforcement.

At the tertiary level, practitioners are working with students who have failed multiple times. It is difficult for students who have experienced repeated failures to be willing to try a new intervention because it poses yet another opportunity for them to experience failure. A positive student–teacher relationship is a foundation for the trust that is necessary for the students to risk failure and buy-in to the proposed intervention. Psychologist Carl Rogers (1995) identified four skills that are useful for building positive relationships with students: empathy, unconditional positive regard, congruence, and active listening.

Empathy

Empathy is about communicating to students that we are aware of what they are feeling. Empathy is nonjudgmental; it is not about whether a student should feel that way or not, it is simply us acknowledging the feeling. For example, when a student pounds on her desk out of frustration because she could not say what she wanted, the teacher could respond with a statement of empathy: "It can be very frustrating when you can't find the words to tell me what you want." Empathy is different from sympathy, when we feel sorry for someone. That is not what students need; instead they need empathy. One final caution when trying to use empathetic statements is to make sure you don't overidentify with the child by saying something like, "I know what you are feeling." Even if we have faced similar struggles, we cannot know for sure what the child is feeling at that moment. To be empathetic, we can imagine what it must be like to live in the student's world, but we can never assume that we know for sure what that world feels like. Teachers can use empathy to communicate to their students that they are aware that things are difficult, frustrating, or just not their favorite thing to do.

Unconditional Positive Regard

Unconditional positive regard is when teachers communicate to students that they accept them for who they are, without judgment. Again, this does not mean we approve of what they do or the choice they make, but we acknowledge them as a person (strengths, weaknesses, and everything in between). Unconditional positive regard may be particularly relevant for students with social difficulties. A sense of acceptance and welcome in a classroom may be a new experience for them, one that can help build a powerful student–teacher bond.

Congruence

Congruence is the consistency between what we say and what we do. This consistency between words and actions/body language can help students who have difficulty reading social cues. It can also be an important component of modeling. If we say something is a key part of social interactions (i.e., not interrupting others) and then fail to follow through with our actions (we consistently interrupt others when they are talking), it will be confusing for the students and make their learning of better skills more difficult.

Active Listening

Active listening is about how we act and respond when students are talking to us. If we sit passively or are distracted when students are talking to us, they may interpret these behaviors as our not being interested in them or not caring about what they have to say. If we are active, we use both verbal and nonverbal communication to let the speaker know that we are paying attention and listening to what he or she has to say. Active listening skills such as eye contact, facing the speaker, getting down on a student's level, nodding our head, or making sounds that indicate interest are several ways we can show the speaker we are actively engaged in what he or she is saying. Another part of active listening is giving the speaker feedback. The listener can do this by reflecting what the speaker said ("What I heard you say was…"), asking questions to clarify understanding, summarizing what the speaker said, and waiting until the speaker is finished before responding. When we do respond, we should think carefully about the content of the message, be respectful, and provide feedback that meets the speaker where he or she is. This last point—of meeting the speaker where he or she is—can be difficult. A student comes to a teacher with a problem, and it is natural to want to solve that problem for the student; however, active listening involves things like identifying when someone is seeking assistance versus when someone just wants to tell someone else what he or she is thinking. When teachers use good active listening skills, they serve as models for students with social deficits. Additionally, these skills can help teachers when they are trying to understand what a child with social difficulties wants or needs.

Finally, the student–teacher relationship can help during intervention planning, as it allows teachers to get to know what students like or dislike, what their skills are like under different conditions, interests, hobbies, and so on.

PLANNING FOR MAINTENANCE AND GENERALIZATION OF SKILLS

In this final section, we discuss some of the assumptions about social skills interventions that are vital to maximizing social validity and generalization of skill gains across settings and contexts of newly developed social competencies. A social skills intervention cannot be valid without the generalization of competencies learned: The social skills acquired by the student must be demonstrated in settings outside of where the intervention takes place. Developing a skill that is only used in a single social situation does not provide a meaningful benefit to students. This is where many of the initial attempts at social skills training failed to demonstrate significant changes that could be sustained over time. They could teach a student an isolated social skill or even set of skills, but the skills never went beyond the initial setting in which they were learned. Planning for generalization and maintenance of skills is an essential part of any evidence-based individual plan, because it is these later plan components that move students from learning social skills to developing broader social competency.

Once skills are consistently being performed in one setting, the intervention plan needs to shift in focus from initial skill development to use of the skills in new

---

A Common Example of Failure to Generalize Skills

One of us (J. S.) has consulted with several different self-contained classrooms for students with emotional and behavior disorders. In one classroom, the students would raise their hands and stay in their seats when the primary teacher was in the classroom. When the teacher left the classroom, disruptions typically occurred that required the involvement of either the team leader or assistant principal. On days where the teacher was out sick, typically one or more of the students in this classroom would end up suspended. This situation put stress on the teacher, who felt so responsible for her students that by the end of the year she never left the classroom and would regularly come into work when she was not feeling well. It was a great first step for these students to demonstrate these skills in the presence of the teacher, but the benefit of this improvement was tied to one specific cue: the teacher. These students needed an intervention plan that went beyond the first step of initial behavior change to generalize their skills to other people and situations.

---

situations, with new people, and developing other related skills. Steps for promoting generalization include (1) conduct skills development and other intervention activities in multiple, natural locations (i.e., reward a student for appropriate interactions in the classroom, on the playground, in the cafeteria, and at assemblies) where students have frequent opportunities to use the skill; (2) once the intervention has been identified as being effective, involve multiple people in the delivery of the intervention (i.e., other teachers, cafeteria workers, bus drivers, and parents); (3) fade external cues or reinforcers; and (4) continue to monitor and evaluate progress. Progress monitoring should continue through the generalization phase just as it did when the intervention was initially being implemented. As the intervention plan shifts from initial behavior change and skills development to generalization, progress monitoring should also shift to these new settings so that the effectiveness of the generalization strategies can be evaluated.

Another aspect of generalization includes the skills that are targeted for improvement. When identifying which skills will be included in the intervention plan, practitioners should look for skills that apply across many different types of situations. One example of a general skill is problem solving. Problem-solving steps, such as (1) identify the problem, (2) analyze the problems, (3) brainstorm possible solutions, (4) choose and try a solution, and (5) evaluate the result, can be taught and reinforced in a variety of different situations. For example, a student could initially be taught problem-solving steps to help him or her work through conflicts in social situations; then those same problem-solving steps could be applied to academic difficulties or beyond the school into the community or home environments.

Parent Training

A key component of any generalization plan is parent training. When parents have the knowledge and skills to support their child's skill development, the transfer of skills from school to home will be significantly increased. In a study conducted by DeRosier and Gilliom (2007), a randomized control design was used to evaluate the value added of including parent training in addition to child training in skills that other research had noted were related to improved social functioning (Crick & Dodge, 1994) in interactions with both adults and peers. The specific skills targeted by this program were teaching students to (1) read social cues accurately; (2) generate, select, and utilize appropriate responses in social situations; and (3) self-regulate (monitoring, evaluating, and correcting) their own emotional responses. They found that students who were in the parent training-only group demonstrated in their knowledge of the three target social skills areas, demonstrating that parents can be effective teachers of social skills.

As with other types of interventions, buy-in and treatment integrity increase the success of parent training interventions. In order for parents to teach and reinforce skill utilization, parents must be committed to the program and follow through on that commitment with regular attendance. For schools to conduct effective parent training, they should start by identifying potential barriers to parent participation such as when and where the session will be held; what the target child as well as any siblings will do during the parent training sessions; and transportation (these latter two being common barriers to parent participation). Additionally, parents could be offered other incentives, such as a meal for the family since many of these sessions occur in the evening during dinnertime. Some skill programs such as Families and Schools Together (McDonald, Billingham, Conrad, Morgan, & Payton, 1997) have combined child training and parent training with group meals, where student and their families had immediate opportunities to practice and receive feedback on the skills they had just learned.

Implementing effective parent training should follow the model of effective school-wide and classroom based programs presented in earlier chapters. Schools should begin by using a combination of research on high-impact skills and skills identified as being important to families (social validity) to decide which to include in the parent training sessions. Once the skills have been identified, schools can draw off the various social curricula presented in previous chapters to design high-quality parent training programs. Often parent training programs are presented to complement the skills instruction students are receiving in school. While parent training alone can help students, this model of combining student and parent training is a better method of promoting generalization, as students are learning, using, and receiving feedback on skills from different people in different environments. As parents implement the skills they have learned, they will need support from a consultant as well as opportunities to receive support from other parents facing the same challenges. Finally, schools should be creative in thinking about how to engage families, remove barriers, and provide meaningful incentives to increase participation and intervention integrity.

Maintenance of Skill Gains

Once students can independently perform skills in different settings or situations, the focus of the intervention plan shifts into the final maintenance stage. During this last phase of the individual intervention plan, (1) supports are faded, (2) responsibility is shifted from the adults to the child, (3) motivation should shift from external to internal, and (4) assessment becomes intermittent. Maintenance plans typically involve intermittent reinforcement delivered on a variable schedule. Some people worry about students becoming dependent on external rewards. If rewards are used to develop skills that are meaningful to students (such as friendship skills), then eventually an internal sense of self-competence and success will make those external motivators irrelevant. This is why long-term motivators that will be used to maintain the skills gains over time should be identified during the initial plan development.

Various strategies can be used to promote the maintenance of skills gains. One method is to promote the development of intrinsic motivation as well as student responsibility for behavior change by increasing self-regulation skills (Zimmerman, 2008). Another feature of maintenance plans include check-in or refresher sessions. These sessions, analogous to booster vaccinations, can help prevent students from relapsing into previous problem behaviors. For students with disabilities, any effective individual intervention plan will include support plans to respond to early signs of relapse. During this maintenance phase, regular progress monitoring is no longer necessary; however, practitioners should put some type of early detection system in place to identify possible signs of relapse or the emergence of new problem behaviors.

SUMMARY AND CONCLUSIONS

This chapter has presented the process of assessment and intervention at the tertiary level for students with intensive social skills needs. We reviewed widely used tools of behavior assessment, team-based frameworks for conducting assessment, areas of intervention, and the importance of generalization. The goal of social skills assessment and intervention is to assist teachers and students in developing not only immediate skills but also lifelong competencies that influence elementary students' social participation in the later grades and beyond. Therefore, we believe best practice to be team-based assessment and implementation coupled with a longitudinal holistic approach to social skills instruction. The following list summarizes key points and final thoughts on designing individual interventions:

✓ Completing all steps in the process is necessary to develop an individual social skills intervention that is evidence based, including assessment, intervention development and implementation, progress monitoring and evaluating intervention effectiveness, and planning for generalization and maintenance of skills. The number and complexity of activities at each step may vary based on the needs and complexity of each student's issues, but the steps do not change. Collecting baseline data, knowing the conditions under which a behavior does or does not occur, monitoring behavior change and the implementation of the intervention, and identifying how to ensure the behavior will continue once the intervention is terminated are just as important for intervention success regardless if the intervention is as easy as a classroom teacher implementing a simple reinforcement system to improve help-seeking behavior or as complex as a team addressing the multiple social deficits of a student with severe autism.

✓ Neither assessment nor intervention should be "one size fits all" at this level. Both assessment tools and interventions should be chosen and utilized based on (1) the availability of evidence to support their quality and (2) how well they match the needs of each specific student.

✓ High-quality professional development is just as important when implementing Tier 3 interventions as it is when implementing interventions at Tier 1 or 2. For an overview of what makes high-quality professional development, see Garet, Porter, Desimone, Birman, and Yoon (2001).

✓ Create a best practices or "what works" resource for your district. All too often in school districts there are creative interventions and success stories that never go beyond the walls of an individual teacher's classroom. Districts should consider constructing a mechanism for school professionals to share successful individual intervention plans. There are many ways that school could approach this task. For example, create a "what works" page on the district intranet where interventions can be posted (leaving out student specifics, of course, to protect confidentiality) or identify a person in the district to collect and maintain an intervention plan reference database that can be searched by student needs or intervention type. Districts can also dedicate one professional development day a year to disseminating successful interventions from within the district. District staff present intervention ideas or best practices case study examples. This approach is low cost for the district, makes employees feel their skills and knowledge are valued, and identifies knowledgeable individuals in the district who can serve as ongoing supports for their peers. Outside experts are useful and can be both informative and inspiring, but often that knowledge and inspiration abate when teachers return to the realities of their classrooms.

✓ Acknowledge and reward successes. Too frequently, it is only the failures that receive attention from administrators. The following is an all too common situation: Staff who have weak skills are sent to off-site training or receive extra support and resources to improve their skills while skilled, successful staff are just given more work. While providing more support and training is the right approach for people who are struggling, districts need to find ways to reinforce expertise.

✓ Using the suggestions and references contained in this chapter, create your own best practices steps to developing individual interventions and use that guide to train key personnel in your district.

The following list summarizes key points on effective interventions:

✓ Intervention decisions are clearly linked to assessment results.

✓ Focus on reinforcing skills rather than punishing problems. Reinforcement builds skills and, therefore, is directly connected to learning and skill development. Punishment, when it works, only eliminates a negative behavior. When that negative behavior is gone, it is usually replaced by another negative.

✓ Combine individual (Tier 3) interventions with peer-mediated, classwide, and universal social skills programs.

✓ Provide opportunities for daily skills instruction and daily practice in regular school situations. Regular practice and feedback as well as opportunities to practice in the natural environment where the skills are used are key to a student using the skills they have been taught (NASP, 2002).

✓ Address environmental factors in the inclusive classroom that impact individual students' abilities to develop and maintain social competencies.

✓ Interventions must take into account individual factors that influence students' learning of appropriate and expected social behaviors (NASP, 2002).

✓ Include all of the adults who interact with a student.

✓ Create a crisis support plan to address any extinction bursts that may occur when the intervention is first put into place.

✓ Change takes time, especially when deficits are severe or behaviors are part of long-standing habits. Interventions need to be given a reasonable amount of time for change to occur. This does not mean that problems in the intervention shouldn't be adjusted, just that too often intervention plans are abandoned before they have had a chance to affect a change in behavior.

✓ For the student with more severe deficits, create an ongoing support plan and a crisis intervention plan that are informed by assessment data and the student's individual behavior plan.

✓ Include in the written intervention sections on generalization and maintenance. In the generalization section, document the specific strategies that will be used to promote the transfer of targeted skills to new people, places, and situations. In the maintenance section, include support plans that can be used in case of crisis or relapse as well as how support will continue to be provided as the student grows and develops. During the maintenance phase, the focus shifts from specific skills to the promotion of broader social competency.

References

Aber, J., Brown, J., & Jones, S. (2003). Developmental trajectories toward violence in middle school childhood: Course, demographic differences, and response to school-based intervention. *Development and Psychology, 39*(2), 324–348.

Aber, J., Pedersen, S., Brown, J., Jones, S., & Gershoff, E. (2003). Changing children's trajectories of development: Two-year evidence for the effectiveness of a school-based approach to violence prevention. Columbia University, Prepared for the National Center for Child in Poverty. Retrieved March 23, 2012, from *www.nccp.org/publications/pub_554.html*.

Ainsworth, M. D. S. (1973). The development of infant–mother attachment. In B. Caldwell & H. Ricciuti (Eds.), *Review of child development research* (Vol. 3, pp. 1–94). Chicago: University of Chicago Press.

Ainsworth, M. D. S. (1979). Infant–mother attachment. *American Psychologist, 34*, 932–937.

Algozzine, K. M., Morsink, C. V., & Algozzine, B. (1986). Classroom ecology in categorical special education classrooms: And so, they counted the teeth in the horse! *Journal of Special Education, 20*, 209–217.

Allport, G. (1954). *The nature of prejudice*. Cambridge, MA: Addison-Wesley.

American Educational Research Association, American Psychological Association, and National Council on Measurement in Education. (1999). *Standards for educational and psychological testing*. Washington, DC : American Psychological Association.

Ames, C., & Ames, R. (1984). Systems of student and teacher motivation: Toward a qualitative definition. *Journal of Educational Psychology, 76*, 535–556.

Bandura, A. (1977). *Social learning theory*. Englewood Cliffs, NJ: Prentice Hall.

Bandura, A. (1999). A social cognitive theory of personality. In L. Pervin & O. John (Eds.), *Handbook of personality* (pp. 154–196). New York: Guilford Press.

Bandura, A., Barbaranelli, C., Caparara, G. V., & Pastorelli, C. (1996). Multifaceted impact of self-efficacy beliefs on academic functioning. *Child Development, 67*, 1206–1222.

Bandura, A., & Walters, R. H. (1963). *Social learning and personality development*. New York: Holt, Rinehart, & Winston.

Beland, K. (1989). *Second Step, grades 4–5: Summary report*. Seattle, WA: Committee for Children.

Beland, K. (1991). *Second Step, preschool–kindergarten: Summary report*. Seattle, WA: Committee for Children.

Bellini, S. (2006). *Building social relationships: A systematic approach to teaching social interactions skills to children and adolescents with autism spectrum disorders and other social difficulties*. Shawnee Mission, KS: Autism Asperger Publishing.

Bergan, J. R. (1995). Evolution of a problem-solving model of consultation. *Journal of Educational and Psychological Consultation, 6*(2), 111–123.

Bergin, C., & Bergin, D. (2009). Attachment in the classroom. *Educational Psychology Review, 21*, 141–170.

Bernard, B. (1993). Fostering resiliency in kids. *Educational Leadership, 51*, 44–48.

Bernard, B. (1995). *Fostering resiliency in kids: Protective factors in the family, school and community*. San Francisco: Far West Laboratory for Educational Research and Development.

Bierman, K., Smoot, D. L., & Aumiller, K. (1993). Characteristics of aggressive-rejected, aggressive (nonrejected), and rejected (nonaggressive) boys. *Child Development*, (1), 139.

Birch, S. H., & Ladd, G. W. (1996). Interpersonal relationships in the school environment and children's early school adjustment: The role of teachers and peers. In J. Jaana & K. R. Wentzel (Eds.), *Social motivation: Understanding children's school adjustment* (pp. 199–225). New York: Cambridge University Press.

Bjorklund, D., Bjorklund, B., Brown, R., & Cassel, W. (1998). Children's susceptibility to repeated questions: How misinformation changes children's answers and their minds. *Applied Developmental Science, 2*, 99–111.

Bowlby, J. (1969). *Attachment and loss: Vol. I. Attachment*. London: Hogarth Press.

Bradshaw, C. P., Koth, C. W., Thornton, L. A., & Leaf, P. J. (2009). Altering school climate through school-wide positive behavioral interventions and supports: Findings from a group-randomized effectiveness trial. *Prevention Science, 10*(2), 100–115.

Bradshaw, C. P., Mitchell, M., & Leaf, P. (2010). Examining the effects of school-wide positive behavioral interventions and supports on student outcomes: Results from a randomized controlled effectiveness trial in elementary schools. *Journal of Positive Behavior Interventions, 12*(3), 133–148.

Bretherton, I., & Munholland, K. (1999). Internal working models in attachment relationships: A construct revisited. In J. Cassidy & P. Shaver (Eds.), *Handbook of attachment: Theory, research, and clinical applications* (pp. 89–111). New York: Guilford Press.

Brown, B. B. (1989). The role of peer groups in adolescents' adjustment to secondary school. In T. J. Berndt & G. W. Ladd (Eds.), *Peer relationships in child development* (pp. 188–215). New York: Wiley.

Brown, B. B., & Lohr, M. J. (1987). Peer group affiliation and adolescent self-esteem: An integration of ego-identity and symbolic interaction theories. *Journal of Personality and Social Psychology, 52*, 47–55.

Brown, L. J., Black, D. D., & Downs, J. C. (1984). *School Social Skills Rating Scale*. New York: Slosson.

Bursuck, W. D., & Asher, S. R. (1986). The relationship between social competence and achievement in elementary school children. *Journal of Clinical Psychology, 15*, 41–49.

Caldarella, P., & Merrell, K. W. (1997). Common dimensions of social skills of children and adolescents: A taxonomy of positive behaviors. *School Psychology Review, 26*, 264–278.

Caprara, G. V., Barbaranelli, C., Pastorelli, C., Bandura, A., & Zimbardo, P. (2000). Psychosocial foundations of children's academic achievement. *Psychological Science, 11*, 302–306.

Children's Services Council of Palm Beach County. (2007, September). *Research review. Evidence-based programs and practices: What does it all mean?* Prepared for Children's Services Council of Palm Beach County, Boynton Beach, FL. Retrieved March 10, 2012, from *www.evidence-basedassociates.com/reports/research_review.pdf.*

Coalition for Evidence-Based Policy. (2003). *Identifying and implementing educational practices supported by rigorous evidence: A user friendly guide.* Washington, DC: U.S. Department of Education, Institute of Education Sciences. Retrieved from *www2.ed.gov/rschstat/research/pubs/rigorousevid/rigorousevid.pdf.*

Cohen, B. P., & Cohen, E. G. (1991). From groupwork among children to R&D teams: Interdependence, interaction and productivity. *Advances in Group Processes, 8,* 205–226.

Cohen, E. G. (1994). *Restructuring the classroom: Conditions for productive small groups* (ERIC Document Reproduction Service No. ED 347 639). Washington, DC: Office of Educational Research and Improvement.

Coie, J. D., Dodge, K. A., & Coppotelli, H. (1982). Dimensions and types of social status: A cross-age perspective. *Developmental Psychology, 19,* 557–570.

Conduct Problems Prevention Research Group. (1999). Initial impact of the Fast Track prevention trial for conduct problems: I. The high-risk sample. *Journal of Consulting and Clinical Psychology, 67,* 631–647.

Conduct Problems Prevention Research Group. (2002). Fast Track Prevention trial: Evaluation through third grade. *Journal of Abnormal Child Psychology, 30,* 1–52.

Conduct Problems Prevention Research Group. (2007). Fast Track randomized controlled trial to prevent externalizing psychiatric disorders: Findings from grades 3 to 9. *Journal of the American Academy of Child and Adolescent Psychiatry, 46*(10), 1250–1262.

Conduct Problems Prevention Research Group. (2010). Fast Track intervention effects on youth arrests and delinquency. *Journal of Experimental Criminology, 6,* 131–157.

Conduct Problems Prevention Research Group. (2011). The effects of the Fast Track preventive intervention on the development of conduct disorder across childhood. *Child Development, 82*(1), 331–345.

Constantino, J. N., & Gruber, C. P. (2005). *Social Responsiveness Scale.* Los Angeles: Western Psychological Services.

Cooke, M. B., Ford, J., Levine, J., Bourke, C., Newell, L., & Lapidus, G. (2007). The effects of city-wide implementation of "Second Step" on elementary school students' prosocial and aggressive behaviors. *Journal of Primary Prevention, 28*(2), 93–115.

Cook, B. G., Tankersley, M., Cook, L., & Landrum, T. (2000). Teacher attitudes toward their included students with disabilities. *Exceptional Children, 67,* 115–135.

Coucouvanis, J. (2005). *Super skills: A social skills group program for children with Asperger syndrome, high-functioning autism and related disorders.* Shawnee Mission, KS: Autism Asperger Publishing.

Cowan, R. J., & Sheridan, S. M. (2003). Investigating the acceptability of behavioral interventions in applied conjoint behavioral consultation: Moving from analog conditions to natural settings. *School Psychology Quarterly, 18*(1), 1–21.

Crick, N. R., & Dodge, K. A. (1994). A review and reformulation of social information-processing mechanisms in children's social adjustment. *Psychological Bulletin, 115,* 74–101.

Curby, T. W., Rudasill, K. M., Rimm-Kaufman, S., & Konold, T. R. (2008). The role of social competence in predicting gifted enrollment. *Psychology in the Schools, 45,* 729–744.

Daly, E. J., III, Witt, J. C., Martens, B. K., & Dool, E. J. (1997). A model for conducting a functional analysis of academic performance problems. *School Psychology Review, 26,* 554–574.

Datnow, A., & Castellano, M. (2000). Teachers' responses to Success for All: How beliefs, experiences, and adaptations shape implementation. *American Educational Research Journal, 37,* 775–799.

Davidson, N. (1985). Small-group learning and teaching in mathematics: A selective review of the research. In R. E. Slavin, S. Saran, S. Kagan, R. Hertz-Lazarowitz, C. Webb, & R. Schmuck (Eds.), *Learning to cooperate, cooperating to learn* (pp. 211–230). New York: Plenum.

Denham, S. (2006). Social-emotional competence as support for school readiness: What is it and how do we assess it? *Early Education and Development, 17,* 57–89.

DeRosier, M. E., & Gilliom, M. (2007). Effectiveness of a parent training program for improving children's social behavior. *Journal of Child and Family Studies, 16,* 660–670.

Desimone, L. (2002). How can comprehensive school reform models be successfully implemented? *Review of Educational Research, 72,* 433–479.

DiPerna, J. C., & Elliott, S. N. (2000). *Academic Competence Evaluation Scales (ACES).* San Antonio, TX: Psychological Corporation.

DiPerna, J. C., & Elliott, S. N. (2002). Promoting academic enablers to improve student achievement: An introduction to mini-series. *School Psychology Review, 31,* 293–297.

Doll, B., & Elliott, S. N. (1994). Representativeness of observed preschool social behaviors: How many data are enough? *Journal of Early Intervention, 18,* 227–238.

Dougherty, M. A., & Dougherty, L. P. (1991). The sources and management of resistance to consultation. *School Counselor, 38,* 178–187.

Dreeben, R. (1968). *On what is learned in school.* London: Addison-Wesley

Durlak, J. A., Weissberg, R. P., Dymnicki, A. B., Taylor, R. D., & Schellinger, K. B. (2011). The impact of enhancing students' social and emotional learning: A meta-analysis of school-based universal interventions. *Child Development, 82,* 405–432.

Elias, M. J., & Haynes, N. M. (2008). Social competence, social support, and academic achievement in minority, low-income, urban elementary school children. *School Psychology Quarterly, 23,* 474–495.

Elliott, S. N. (1988). Acceptability of behavioral treatments in educational settings. In J. C. Witt, S. N. Elliot, & F. M. Gresham (Eds.), *Handbook of behavior therapy in education* (pp. 121–150). New York: Plenum.

Elliott, S. N. (1995). *Final evaluation report: The Responsive Classroom Approach: Its effectiveness and acceptability.* Washington, DC: Author.

Elliott, S. N., Barnard, J., & Gresham, F. M. (1989). Preschoolers' social behavior: Teachers' and parents' assessments. *Journal of Psychoeducational Assessment, 7,* 223–234.

Elliott, S. N., & Busse, R. T. (1991). Social skills assessment and intervention with children and adolescents: Guidelines for assessment and training procedures. *School Psychology International, 12,* 63–83.

Elliott, S. N., DiPerna, J. C., & Shapiro, E. S. (2001). *AIMS: Academic Intervention Monitoring System.* San Antonio, TX: Psychological Corporation.

Elliott, S. N., & Gresham, F. M. (1987). Children's social skills: Assessment and classification practices. *Journal of Counseling and Development, 66,* 96–99.

Elliott, S. N., & McKinnie, D. M. (1994). Relationships and differences among social skills, problem behavior, and academic competence for mainstreamed learning-disabled and non-handicapped students. *Canadian Journal of School Psychology, 10,* 1–14.

Ellis, A. K., & Fouts, J. T. (1993). *Research on educational innovations.* Princeton Junction, NJ: Eye on Education.

Evans, G. W., & Lovell, B. (1979). Design modification in an open-plan school. *Journal of Educational Psychology, 7*(1), 41–49.

Fantuzzo, J., Perry, M. A., & McDermott, P. (2004). Preschool approaches to learning and their relationship to other relevant classroom competencies for low-income children. *School Psychology Quarterly, 19*(3), 212–230.

Feldhusen, J. F., Thurston, J. R., & Benning, J. J. (1970). Longitudinal analysis of classroom behavior and school achievement. *Journal of Experimental Education, 38*(4), 4–10.

Ferguson, A. A. (2001). *Bad boys: Public schools in the making of black masculinity.* Ann Arbor: University of Michigan Press.

Ford, M. E. (1982). Social cognition and social competence in adolescence. *Developmental Psychology, 18,* 323–340.

Ford, M. E. (1985). The concept of competence: Themes and variations. In H. A. Marlowe, Jr., & R. B. Weinberg (Eds.), *Competence development* (pp. 3–49). New York: Academic Press.

Ford, M. E. (1987). Processes contributing to adolescent social competence. In M. E. Ford & D. H. Ford (Eds.), *Humans as self-constructing living systems: Putting the framework to work* (pp. 199–233). Hillsdale, NJ: Erlbaum.

Ford, M. E. (1992). *Motivating humans.* Newbury Park, CA: Sage.

Ford, M. E., Wentzel, K. R., Wood, D. N., Stevens, E., & Siesfeld, G. A. (1989). Processes associated with integrative social competence: Emotional and contextual influences on adolescent social responsibility. *Journal of Adolescent Research, 4,* 405–425.

Friend, M., & Cook, L. (2010). *Interactions: Collaboration skills for school professional* (6th ed.). Needham Heights, MA: Allyn & Bacon.

Galindo, C., & Fuller, B. (2010). The social competence of Latino kindergartners and growth in mathematical understanding. *Developmental Psychology, 46,* 579–592.

Garet, M. S., Porter, A. C., Desimone, L. Birman, B. F., & Yoon, K. S. (2001). What makes professional development effective? Results from a national sample of teachers *American Educational Research Journal, 38,* 915–945.

Gest, S. D., Sesma, A., Masten, A. S., & Tellegen, A. (2006). Childhood peer reputation as a predictor of competence and symptoms 10 years later. *Journal of Abnormal Child Psychology, 34,* 507–524.

Green, K. D., Forehand, R., Beck, S., & Vosk, B. (1980). An assessment of the relationship among measures of children's social competence and children's academic achievement. *Child Development, 51,* 1149–1156.

Greenberg, M. (2012). *Summary of findings on the PATHS® curriculum.* Pennsylvania State University, Prepared for Channing-Bete Company. Retrieved March, 14, 2012, from *www.prevention.psu.edu/projects/PATHSFindings.html.*

Gresham, F. M. (1981). Social skills training with handicapped children: A review. *Review of Educational Research, 51,* 139–176.

Gresham, F. M. (1992). Social skills and learning disabilities: Causal, concomitant, or correlational. *School Psychology Review, 21,* 348–360.

Gresham, F. M. (1998). Social skills training: Should we raze, remodel, or rebuild? *Behavioral Disorders, 24,* 19–25.

Gresham, F. M., Dolstra, L., Lambros, K. M., McLaughlin, V., & Lane, K. L. (2000, November). *Teacher expected model behavior profiles: Changes over time.* Paper presented at the Teacher Educators for Children with Behavioral Disorders Conference, Scottsdale, AZ.

Gresham, F. M., & Elliott, S. N. (1990). *Social Skills Rating System.* Circle Pines, MN: American Guidance Service.

Gresham, F. M., & Elliott, S. N. (2008). *Social Skills Improvement System (SSIS).* Upper Saddle River, NJ: Pearson Assessments.

Gresham, F. M., Sugai, G., & Horner, R. H. (2001). Interpreting outcomes of social skills training for students with high-incidence disabilities. *Exceptional Children, 67,* 331–344.

Grossman, D. C., Neckerman, H. J., Koepsell, T. D., Liu, P. Y., Asher, K. N., Beland, K., et al. (1997). Effectiveness of a violence prevention curriculum among children in elementary school: A randomized control trial. *Journal of the American Medical Association, 277,* 1605–1611.

Guardino, C. A., & Fullerton, F. (2010). Changing behaviors by changing the classroom environment. *Teaching Exceptional Children, 42*(6), 8–13.

Haggerty, R. J., Sherrod, L. R., Garmezy, N., & Rutter, M. (1994). *Stress, risk, and resilience in children and adolescents: Processes, mechanisms, and interventions.* New York: Cambridge University Press.

Hampton, V. R., & Fantuzzo, J. W. (2003). The validity of the Penn Interactive Peer Play Scale with urban, low-income kindergarten children. *School Psychology Review, 32*, 77–91.

Hartup, W. W. (1983). Peer relations. In P. H. Mussen (Ed.), *Handbook of child psychology* (Vol. 4, pp. 104–196). New York: Wiley.

Hastings, R. P., & Graham, S. (1995). Adolescents' perception of young people with severe difficulties: The effects of integration schemes and frequency of contact. *Educational Psychology, 15*(2), 149–159.

Henricsson, L., & Rydell, A. (2006). Children with behaviour problems: The influence of social competence and social relations on problem stability, school achievement and peer acceptance across the first six years of school. *Infant and Child Development, 15*, 347–366.

Hersh, R. H., & Walker, H. M. (1983). Great expectations: Making schools effective for all students. *Policy Studies Review, 2*(1), 47–188.

Hintze, J. M., Stoner, G., & Bull, M. H. (2000). Analogue assessment: Emotional/behavioral problems. In E. S. Shapiro & T. R. Kratochwill (Eds.), *Conducting school-based assessment of student and adolescent behaviors* (pp. 21–54). New York: Guilford Press.

Hood-Smith, N. E., & Leffingwell, R. J. (1983). The impact of physical space alternation on disruptive classroom behavior: A case study. *Education, 104*, 224–231.

Horsch, P., Chen, J., & Nelson, D. (1999). Rules and rituals: Tools for creating a respectful, caring learning community. *Phi Delta Kappan, 81*(3), 223–227.

Howes, C. (2000). Socio-emotional climate in child care, teacher-child relationships and children's second grade peer relations. *Child Development, 61*, 2004–2021.

Hurley, J. J., Wehby, J. H., & Feurer, I. D. (2010). The social validity assessment of social competence intervention behavior goals. *Topics in Early Childhood Special Education, 30*, 112–124.

Iwata, B. A., Dorsey, M. F., Slifer, K. J., Bauman, K. E., & Richman, G. S. (1994). Toward a functional analysis of self-injury. *Journal of Applied Behavior Analysis, 27*, 197–209. (Reprinted from *Analysis and Intervention in Development Disabilities, 2*, 3–20, 1982)

Jackson, P. W. (1968). *Life in classrooms.* New York: Holt, Rinehart, & Winston.

Jones, R. R., Reid, J. B., & Patterson, G. R. (1979). Naturalistic observation in clinical assessment. In P. McReynolds (Ed.), *Advances in psychological assessment* (Vol. 3, pp. 42–95). San Francisco: Jossey-Bass.

Kaderavek, J. N. (2011). *Language disorders in children: Fundamental concepts of assessment and intervention.* Upper Saddle River, NJ: Pearson.

Kazdin, A. E. (1980). Acceptability of alternative treatments for deviant child behavior. *Journal of Applied Behavior Analysis, 13*, 259–273.

Kerr, M. M., & Zigmond, N. (1986). What do high school teachers want? A study of expectations and standards. *Education and Treatment of Children, 9*, 239–249.

Kilian, J. M., Fish, M. C., & Maniago, E. B. (2006). Making school safe: A system-wide school intervention to increase student prosocial behaviors and enhance school climate. *Journal of Applied School Psychology, 23*(1), 1–30.

Kirby, L. D., & Fraser, M. W. (1997). Risk and resilience in childhood. In M. W. Fraser (Ed.), *Risk and resilience in childhood: An ecological perspective* (pp. 10–33). Washington, DC: NASW Press.

Knoff, H. M., & Batsche, G. M. (1995). Project ACHIEVE: Analyzing a school reform process for at-risk and underachieving students. *School Psychology Review, 24*(4), 579–603.

Kol'tsova, V. A. (1978). Experimental study of cognitive activity in communication (with specific reference to concept formation). *Soviet Psychology, 17*(1), 23–38.

Kratochwill, T. R., & Bergan, J. R. (1990). *Behavioral consultation in applied settings: An individual guide.* New York: Plenum.

Kupersmidt, J. B., & Coie, J. D. (1990). Preadolescent peer status, aggression, and school adjustment as predictors of externalizing problems in adolescence. *Child Development, 61,* 1350–1362.

Kupersmidt, J. B., Coie, J. D., & Dodge, K. A. (1990). The role of poor peer relationships in the development of disorder. In S. R. Asher & J. D. Coie (Eds.), *Peer rejection in childhood* (pp. 274–305). New York: Cambridge University Press.

Kusché, C. A., & Greenberg, M. T. (1994). *The PATHS curriculum.* Seattle: Developmental Research and Programs.

Ladd, G. W. (1990). Having friends, keeping friends, making friends, and being liked by peers in the classroom: Predictors of children's early school adjustment? *Child Development, 61,* 1091–1100.

Ladd, G. W. (1999). Peer relationships and social competence during early and middle childhood. *Annual Review of Psychology, 50,* 333–359.

Ladd, G. W., & Burgess, K. B. (1999). Charting the relationship trajectories of aggressive, withdrawn, and aggressive/withdrawn children during early grade school. *Child Development, 70,* 1344–1367.

Lambert, N. M. (1972). Intellectual and non-intellectual predictors of high school status. *Journal of Special Education, 6,* 247–259.

Lane, K. L., Givner, C. C., & Pierson, M. R. (2004). Teacher expectation's of student behavior: Social skills necessary for success in elementary school classrooms. *Journal of Special Education, 38,* 104–110.

Lane, K. L., Pierson, M. R., & Givner, C. C. (2003). Teacher expectations of student behavior: Which skills do elementary and secondary teachers deem necessary for success in the classroom. *Education and Treatment of Children, 26,* 413–430.

Lane, K. L., Pierson, M. R., & Givner, C. C. (2004). Secondary teachers' views on social competence: Skills essential for success. *Journal of Special Education, 38,* 174–186.

Lane, K. L., Wehby, J. H., & Cooley, C. (2006). Teacher expectations of students' classroom behavior across the grade span: Which social skills are necessary for success? *Exceptional Children, 72,* 153–167.

La Paro, K.M., & Pianta, R.C. (2000). Predicting children's competence in the early school years: A meta-analytic review. *Review of Educational Research, 70,* 443–484.

Lassen, S. R., Steele, M. M., & Sailor, W. (2006). The relationship of school-wide positive behavior support to academic achievement in an urban middle school. *Psychology in the Schools, 43*(6), 701–712.

LeBuffe, P.A., Shapiro, V.B., & Naglieri, J.A. (2009). *Devereux Student Strengths Assessment: A measure of social-emotional competencies of children in kindergarten through eighth grade.* Lewisville, NC: Kaplan Early Learning.

Lennox, D. B., & Miltenberger, R. G. (1990). On the conceptualization of treatment acceptability. *Education and Training in Mental Retardation, 25,* 211–224.

Lewis, T. (n.d.). *School-wide positive behavior supports: Implications for special educators.* Retrieved June 1, 2012, from *www.pbis.org/presentations/default.aspx.*

Losen, D. J., & Orfield, G. (2002). *Racial inequity in special education.* Cambridge, MA: Harvard Education Press.

Lou, Y., Abrami, P. C., Spence, J. C., Poulsen, C., Chambers, B., & d'Apollonia, S. (1996). Within-class grouping: A meta-analysis. *Review of Educational Research, 66,* 423–458.

Maccoby, E. E., & Martin, J. A. (1983). Socialization in the context of the family: Parenting-child interaction. In P. H. Mussen & E. M. Hetherington (Eds.), *Handbook of child psychology. Vol. 4: Socialization, personality, and social development* (pp. 1–101). New York: Wiley.

Madden, N. A., & Slavin, R. E. (1983). Effects of cooperative learning on the social acceptance of mainstreamed academically handicapped students. *Journal of Special Education, 17,* 171–182.

Manning, M. L., & Lucking, R. (1991). The what, why, and how of cooperative learning. *Social Studies, 82,* 120–124.

Márquez, P., Martín, R., & Brackett, M. A. (2006). Relating emotional intelligence to social competence and academic achievement in high school students. *Psicothema, 18,* 118–123.

Martin, R. P. (1988). *Assessment of personality and behavior problems.* New York: Guilford Press.

Masten, A.S. (1994). Resilience in individual development: Successful adaptation despite risk and adversity. In M. C. Wang & E. W. Gordon (Eds.), *Educational resilience in inner-city American: Challenges and prospects* (pp. 3–25). Hillsdale, NJ: Erlbaum.

Mayer, M. J., Van Acker, R., Lochman, J., & Gresham, F. M. (2011). *Cognitive-behavioral interventions for emotional and behavioral disorders: School-based practice.* New York: Guilford Press.

McClelland, M. M., Acock, A. C., & Morrison, F. J. (2006). The impact of kindergarten learning-related skills on academic trajectories at the end of elementary school. *Early Childhood Research Quarterly, 21,* 471–490.

McDonald, L., Billingham, S., Conrad, T., Morgan, A., & Payton, E. (1997). Families and Schools Together (FAST): Integrating community development with clinical strategies. *Families in Society, 78*(2), 140–155.

McDougall, P., Hymel, S., Vaillancourt, T., & Mercer, L. (2001). The consequences of childhood peer rejection. In M. R. Leary (Ed.), *Interpersonal rejection* (pp. 213–247). New York: Oxford University Press.

McGinnis, E. (2011). *Skillstreaming the elementary school child: A guide for teaching prosocial skills* (3rd ed.). Champaign, IL: Research Press.

Merrell, K. W. (1999). *Behavioral, social, and emotional assessment of children and adolescents.* Mahwah, NJ: Erlbaum.

Merrell, K. W. (2000). Informant report: Rating scale measures. In E. S. Shapiro & T. R. Kratochwill (Eds.), *Conducting school-based assessment of student and adolescent behaviors* (pp. 203–234). New York: Guilford Press.

Merrell, K. W. (2001). Assessment of children's social skills: Recent developments, best practices, and new directions. *Exceptionality, 9*(1–2), 3–18.

Merrell, K. W. (2002). *School Social Behavior Scales* (2nd ed.). Eugene, OR: Assessment-Intervention Resources.

Merrell, K. W. (2003). *Behavioral, social, and emotional assessment of children and adolescents* (2nd ed.). Mahwah, NJ: Erlbaum.

Merrell, K. W. (2011). *SEARS: Social and Emotional Assets and Resiliency Scales.* Lutz, FL: PAR.

Merrell, K. W., & Gimpel, G. A. (1998). *Social skills of children and adolescents: Conceptualization, assessment, treatment.* Mahwah, NJ: Erlbaum.

Meyer, L. H., Minondo, S., Fisher, M., Larson, M. J., Dunmore, S., Black, J. W., et al. (1998). Frames of friendship: Social relationships among adolescents with diverse abilities. In L. Meyer, H. S. Park, M. Grenot-Scheyer, I. Schwartz, & B. Harry (Eds.), *Making friends: The influences of culture and development* (pp. 189–221). Baltimore: Brookes.

Michelson, L., Sugai, D. P., Wood, R. P., & Kazdin, A. E. (1983). *Social skills assessment and training with children: An empirically based approach.* New York: Plenum.

Mittenberger, R. G. (2012). *Behavior modification: Principles and procedures* (5th ed). Belmont, CA: Wadsworth Cengage Learning.

Mize, J., & Ladd, G. W. (1988). Predicting preschoolers' peer behavior and status from their interpersonal strategies: A comparison of verbal and enactive responses to hypothetical social dilemmas. *Developmental Psychology, 24,* 782–788.

Molloy, L. E., Gest, S. D., & Rulison, K. L. (2011). Peer influences on academic motivation: Exploring multiple methods of assessing youths' most "influential" peer relationships. *Journal of Early Adolescence, 31*(1), 13–40.

Moore, B., & Beland, K. (1992). *Evaluation of Second Step, preschool–kindergarten: A violent prevention curriculum kit. Summary report.* Seattle WA: Committee for Children.

Murray-Harvey, R. (2010). Relationship influences on students' academic achievement, psychological health, and well-being at school. *Educational and Child Psychology, 27*(1), 104–115.

National Association of School Psychologists (NASP). (2002). *Social skills: Promoting positive behavior, academic success, and school safety.* Retrieved August 18, 2012, from *www.nasponline.org/resources/factsheets/socialskills_fs.aspx.*

Ness, B. M., & Middleton, M. J. (2012). A framework for implementing individualized self-regulated learning strategies in the classroom. *Intervention in School and Clinic, 47,* 267–275.

Newcomb, A. F., & Bukowski, W. M. (1983). Social impact and social preference as determinants of children's peer group status. *Developmental Psychology, 19*(6), 856–867.

Newman, R. S. (1991). Goals and self-regulated learning: What motivates children to seek academic help? In M. L. Maehr & P. R. Pintrich (Eds.), *Advances in motivation and achievement* (Vol. 7, pp. 151–183). Greenwich, CT: JAI Press.

Newman, R. S. (2000). Social influences on the development of children's adaptive help seeking: The role of parents, teachers, and peers. *Developmental Review, 20,* 350–404.

Noddings, N. (1989). Theoretical and practical concerns about small groups in mathematics. *Elementary School Journal, 89,* 607–623.

Norcross, J. C., Krebs, P. M., & Prochaska, J. O. (2011). Stages of change. *Journal of Clinical Psychology, 67*(2), 143–154.

Nowicki, E. A. (2003). A meta-analysis of the social competence of children with learning disabilities compared to classmates of low and average to high achievement. *Learning Disability Quarterly, 26*(3), 171–188.

O'Neill, R. E., Horner, R. H., Albin, R. W., Sprague, J. R., Storey, K., & Newton, J. S. (1997). *Functional assessment and program development for problem behavior: A practical handbook* (2nd ed.). Pacific Grove, CA: Brooks/Cole.

Parker, J. G., & Asher, S. R. (1987). Peer relations and later personal adjustment: Are low-accepted children at risk? *Psychological Bulletin, 102,* 357–389.

Parker, J. G., Rubin, K. H., Price, J. M., & DeRosier, M. E. (1995). Peer relationships, child development and adjustment: A developmental psychopathology perspective. In D. Cicchetti & D. J. Cohen (Eds.), *Developmental psychopathology: Risk, disorder, and adaptation* (Vol. 2, pp. 96–161). New York: Wiley.

Paul, R. (2001). *Language disorders from infancy through adolescence: Assessment and intervention.* New York: Mosby.

Phillips, M., & Gross, A. M. (2010). Children. In D. L. Segal & M. Hersen (Eds.), *Diagnostic interviewing* (pp. 423–441). New York: Springer.

Phillips, V., & McCullough, L. (1990). Consultation-based programming: Instituting the collaborative ethic. *Exceptional Children, 56,* 291–304.

Pianta, R. C., Steinberg, M., & Rollins, K. (1995). The first two years of school: Teacher-child relationships and deflections in children's classroom adjustment. *Development and Psychopathology, 7,* 295–312.

Quill, K. (2000). *Do–watch–listen–say: Social and communication intervention for children with autism.* Baltimore: Brookes.

Rasheed, S. A., Fore, C., & Miller, S. (2006). Person-centered planning: Practices, promises, and provisos. *Journal for Vocational Special Needs Education, 28*(3), 47–59.

Ray, C. E., & Elliott, S. N. (2006). Social adjustment and academic achievement: A predictive model for students with diverse academic and behavior competencies. *School Psychology Review, 35,* 493–501.

Reynhout, G., & Carter, M. (2006). Social stories for children with disabilities. *Journal of Autism and Developmental Disorders, 36,* 445–469.

Reynolds, C. R., & Kamphaus, R. W. (2004). *BASC-2: Behavior Assessment System for Children* (2nd ed.). Upper Saddle River, NJ: Pearson.

Rimm-Kaufman, S. E., Fan, X., Chiu, Y.-J., & You, W. (2007). The contribution of the Responsive Classroom Approach on children's academic achievement: Results from a three year longitudinal study. *Journal of School Psychology, 45,* 401–421.

Rimm-Kaufman, S. E., Pianta, R. C., & Cox, M. J. (2000). Teachers' judgments of problems in the transition to kindergarten. *Early Childhood Research Quarterly, 15*(2), 147–166.

Rimm-Kaufman, S. E., & Sawyer, B. E. (2004). Primary-grade teachers' self-efficacy beliefs, attitudes toward teaching, and discipline and teaching practice priorities in relation to the "Responsive Classroom" approach. *The Elementary School Journal, 104*(4), 321–341.

Roberts, C., & Zubrick, S. (1993). Factors influencing the social status of children with mild academic disabilities in regular classrooms. *Exceptional Children, 59,* 192–202.

Rogers, C. (1995). *On becoming a person.* Boston: Houghton Mifflin.

Roorda, D. L., Koomen, H. Y., Split, J. L., & Oort, F. J. (2001). The influence of affective student–teacher relationships on students' school engagements and achievement: A meta-analytic approach. *Review of Educational Research, 81*(4), 493–529.

Rutherford, L. E., Dupaul, G. J., & Jitendra, A. K. (2008). Examining the relationship between treatment outcomes for academic achievement and social skills in school-age children with attention-deficit/hyperactivity disorder. *Psychology in the Schools, 45*(2), 145–157.

Saarni, C. (1999). The development of emotional competence: Pathways to helping children become emotionally competent. In R. Bar-On, J. G. Maree, & M. J. Elias (Eds.), *Educating people to be emotionally intelligent* (pp. 15–36). New York: Praeger.

Saarni, C. (2007). *The development of emotional competence.* New York: Guilford Press.

Sameroff, A. J., & Fiese, B. H. (2000). Transactional regulation: The developmental ecology of early intervention. In S. Meisels & J. Shonkoff (Eds.), *Early intervention: A handbook of theory, practice, and analysis* (pp. 135–159). New York: Cambridge University Press.

Schloss, P. J., & Schloss M. A. (1998). *Applied behavior analysis in the classroom.* Needham Heights, MA: Allyn & Bacon.

Schultz, L. H., Yeates, K. O., & Selman, R. L. (1989). *The Interpersonal Negotiation Strategies Interview: A Scoring Manual.* Cambridge, MA: Harvard Graduate School of Education.

Seifer, R., Gouley, K., Miller, A. L., & Zakriski, A. (2004). Implementation of the PATHS curriculum in an urban elementary school. *Early Education and Development, 15,* 471–486.

Sheridan, S. M., & Walker, D. (1999). Social skills in context: Considerations for assessment, intervention, and generalization. In C. R. Reynolds & T. B. Gutkin (Eds.), *The handbook of school psychology* (3rd ed., pp. 686–708). New York: Wiley.

Shonkoff, J., & Phillips, D. (2000). *From neurons to neighborhoods: The science of early childhood development.* Washington, DC: National Academy Press.

Sieber, R. T. (1979). Classmates as workmates: Informal peer activity in the elementary school. *Anthropology and Education Quarterly, 10,* 207–235.

Simeonsson, R. J., Carlson, D., Huntington, G., McMillen, J., & Brent, L. (2001). Students with disabilities: A national survey of participation in school activities. *Disability and Rehabilitation, 23*(2), 49–63.

Skinner, C. H., Rhymer, K. N., & McDaniel, E. C. (2000). Naturalistic direct observation in educational settings. In E. S. Shapiro & T. R. Kratochwill (Eds.), *Conducting school-based assessment of student and adolescent behaviors* (pp. 21–54). New York: Guilford Press.

Slavin, R. E. (1983). When does cooperative learning increase student achievement? *Psychological Bulletin, 94*, 429–445.

Slavin, R. E. (1984). Team assisted individualization: Cooperative learning and individualized instruction in the mainstreamed classroom. *Remedial & Special Education, 5*(6), 33–42.

Slavin, R. E. (1995). *Cooperative learning: Theory, research, and practice* (2nd ed.). Needham Heights, MA: Allyn & Bacon.

Smith, L. J., Maxwell, S., Lowther, D., Hacker, D., Bol, L., & Nunnery J. (1997). Activities in schools and programs experiencing the most, and least, early implementation successes. *School Effectiveness and School Improvement, 8*(1), 125–150.

Smith, L. J., Ross, S., McNelis, M., Squires, M., Wasson, R., Maxwell, S., et al. (1998). The Memphis restructuring initiative: Analysis of activities and outcomes that impact implementation success. *Education and Urban Society, 30*(3), 276–325.

Steedly, K. M., Schwartz, A., Levin, M., & Luke, S. D. (2008). Social skills and academic achievement. *Evidence for Education, 3*(2), 1–8.

Stephens, T. M., & Arnold, K. D. (1992). *Social Behavior Assessment Inventory: Professional manual.* Odessa, FL: Psychological Assessment Resources.

Strauss, C., & Quinn, N. (1997). *A cognitive theory of cultural meaning.* Cambridge, UK: Cambridge University Press.

Sugai, G., & Horner, R. H. (2008). What we know and need to know about preventing problem behavior in schools. *Exceptionality, 16*, 67–77.

Thijs, J., & Verkuyten, M. (2009). Students' anticipated situational engagement: The roles of teacher behavior, personal engagement, and gender. *Journal of Genetic Psychology, 170*, 268–286.

Thompson, D., Whitney, I., & Smith, P. K. (1994). Bullying of children with special needs in mainstream schools. *Support for Learning, 9*(3), 103–106.

Tobin, T., & Sugai, G. (1996). Patterns in middle school discipline records. *Journal of Emotional and Behavioral Disorders, 4*, 82–95.

Tudge, J. (1992). Vygotsky, the zone of proximal development, and peer collaboration: Implications for classroom practice. In L. C. Moll (Ed.), *Vygotsky and education: Instructional implications and applications of sociohistorical psychology* (pp. 155–172). New York: Cambridge University Press.

U.S. Department of Education, Institute of Education Sciences, & National Center for Education Evaluation and Regional Assistance. (2004, November). *Identifying and implementing educational practices supported by rigorous evidence: A user friendly guide.* Retrieved January 20, 2012, from *www2.ed.gov/rschstat/research/pubs/rigorousevid/index.html.*

Valente, E. (1994). *Home Interview with Child Technical Report.* Technical Report. Vanderbilt University, Nashville, TN.

Vaughn, S., Haager, D., Hogan, A., & Kouzekanani, K. (1992). Self-concept and peer acceptance in students with learning disabilities: A four- to five-year prospective study. *Journal of Educational Psychology, 84*(1), 43–50.

Vaughn, S., McIntosh, R., & Spencer-Rowe, J. (1991). Peer rejection is a stubborn thing: Increasing peer acceptance of rejected students with learning disabilities. *Learning Disabilities Research & Practice, 6*(2), 83–88.

Visser, J. (2001). Aspects of physical provision for pupils with emotional and behavioural difficulties. *Support for Learning, 16*(2), 64–68.

Vollmer, T., & Northup, J. (1996). Some implications of functional analysis for school psychology. *School Psychology Quarterly, 11*, 76–92.

Waasdorp, T. E., Bradshaw, C. P., & Leaf, P. J. (2012). The impact of school-wide positive behavioral interventions and supports (SWPBIS) on bullying and peer rejection: A randomized controlled effectiveness trial. *Archives of Pediatrics and Adolescent Medicine, 116*(2), 149–156.

Wagner, M., Newman, L., Cameto, R., Levine, P., & Marder, C. (2007). *Perceptions and expectations of youth with disabilities: A special topic report of findings from the National Longitudinal Transition Study–2 (NLTS2)* (NCSER 2007-3006). Menlo Park, CA: SRI International.

Walker, H. M., & McConnell, S. (1995). *Walker–McConnell scale of social competence and school adjustment, elementary version.* San Diego, CA: Singular.

Wallach, G. P. (2008). *Language intervention for school-age students: Setting goals for academic success.* New York: Mosby.

Wang, M. C., Haertel, G. D., & Walberg, H. J. (1997). Fostering resilience: What do we know? *Principal, 77*(2), 18–20.

Warren, A. R., Woodall, C. E., Thomas, M., Nunno, M., Keeney, J. M., Larson, S. M., et al. (1999). Assessing the effectiveness of a training program for interviewing child witnesses. *Applied Developmental Science, 3*, 128–135.

Weinstein, C. S. (1979). The physical environment of the school: A review of research. *Review of Educational Research, 49*, 577–610.

Wentzel, K. R. (1991). Relations between social competence and academic achievement in early adolescence. *Child Development, 62*, 1066–1078.

Wentzel, K. R. (1993). Does being good make the grade? Social behavior and academic competence in middle school. *Journal of Educational Psychology, 85*, 357–364.

Wentzel, K. R. (1998). Social relationships and motivation in middle school: The role of parents, teachers, and peers. *Journal of Educational Psychology, 90*, 202–209.

Wentzel, K. R. (1999). Social-motivational processes and interpersonal relationships: Implications for understanding students' academic success. *Journal of Educational Psychology, 91*, 76–97.

Wentzel, K. R., & Caldwell, K. (1997). Friendships, peer acceptance, and group membership: Relations to academic achievement in middle school. *Child Development, 68*, 1198–1209.

Wentzel, K. R., Feldman, S. S., & Weinberger, D. A. (1991). Parental childrearing and academic achievement in boys: The mediational role of socioemotional adjustment. *Journal of Early Adolescence, 11*, 321–339.

Wertsch, J. (1988). *Vygotsky and the social formation of the mind.* Cambridge, MA: Harvard University Press.

Whitaker, P. (1994). Mainstream students talk about integration. *British Journal of Special Education, 21*(1), 13–16.

Whitney, I., Nabuzoka, D., & Smith, P. K. (1992). Bullying in schools: Mainstream and special needs. *Support for Learning, 7*(1), 3–7.

Wilder, D. A., Atwell, J., & Wine, B. (2006). The effects of varying levels of treatment integrity on child compliance during treatment with a three-step prompting procedure. *Journal of Applied Behavior Analysis, 39*, 369–373.

Wilson, H. K., Pianta, R. C., & Stuhlman, M. (2007). Typical classroom experiences in first grade: The role of classroom climate and functional risk in the development of social competencies. *Elementary School Journal, 108*(2), 81–96.

Witt, J. C., & Elliott, S. N. (1985). Acceptability of classroom intervention strategies. *Advances in School Psychology, 4*, 251–288.

Wright, M. O., & Masten, A. S. (2005). Resilience processes and development. In S. Goldstein & R. Brooks (Eds.), *Handbook of resilience in children* (pp. 17–38). New York: Kluwer.

Zimmerman, B. J. (2008). Investigating self-regulation and motivation: Historical background, methodological developments, and future prospects. *American Educational Research Journal, 45*(1), 166–183.

Zsolnai, A. (2002). Relationship between children's social competence, learning motivation and school achievement. *Educational Psychology, 22*, 317–329.

Index

An *f* following a page number indicates a figure; an *n* following a page number indicates a note; a *t* following a page number indicates a table.